STANDING ON THE PROMISES
AND
CLEANING UP THE PREMISES
(PERSONAL AND SOCIAL RELIGION)

by
W. MERLIN SCHWEIN, A.B., B.D., M.DIV., D.D.

*To Norma Sue, with best
wishes from

W. Merlin Schwein*

I.S.B.N. #0932970427

Printed in the United States of America
by
PRINIT PRESS
Dublin, Indiana

DEDICATION

To the members of all the churches I have served as Pastor and District Superintendent who have made an inestimable contribution to my ministry.

INTRODUCTION

This book on personal and social religion has been written because, after 47 years in the ministry, I feel strongly that an attempt should be made to set straight some of what I consider to be misconceptions in religion. These misconceptions, I feel, have been and are still hindrances to the Christian faith and the mission of the Church. These misconceptions are outlined in the first chapter and are treated in depth in the following chapters.

Scripture references are from the Revised Standard version, unless otherwise noted.

Acknowledgments: Dr. Charles Merrill Smith, author and minister friend of many years; Dr. Robert H. Ferrell, Professor of History in Indiana University, author of many books, the most recent a book on former President Trumen in commemoration of the 100th anniversary of his birth; Rev. William M. Schwein, my minister son; all of whom I owe a great debt of gratitude for their help in the preparation of this manuscript.

TABLE OF CONTENTS

I

HIS KINGDOM TARRIES LONG[1]
(Hindrances to the Christian Faith and the Mission of the Church)

In both Matthew's and Luke's Gospels Jesus's plaintive words are quoted: "O Jerusalem, Jerusalem, killing the prophets and stoning those who are sent to you! How often would I have gathered your children together as a hen gathers her brood under her wings, and you would not!" (Luke 13:34). This points up not only the hindrances to the Gospel in Jesus's day but also that the same obstacles exist today and stand in the way of Christ's purpose and the mission of the church.

The problem lies not only with the lay people, but with pastors as well. After six years as a District Superintendent in the Methodist Church, I have far more sympathy for the laity than I had before, as I observed some of the very poor pastoral leadership. Of course, we have effective lay people and effective pastors, but we have many of each who are not. In some cases, this is the result of lack of knowledge; in other cases, it is because of a lack of understanding of the mission of the church. Inept pastoral leadership and ignorance of the laity are the biggest stumbling blocks. Many of the lay people are suspicious of any pastor who is concerned with social evils and are concerned only with personal religion and that, many times, only a very narrow kind.

In the First Chapter, I am attempting to outline some of the wrong ideas of religion which have hindered the mission of the church in the past and which persist yet today. I believe that our Lord would, today, speak words about the church

---

[1]The title is from the hymn "Rise Up, O Men of God" by William P. Merrill.

and His followers which are much the same as He spoke when He was engaged in His earthly ministry. In *The Interpreter's Bible*, in the explanation of Luke 13:34, 35, the writer states: "Here and now the choice confronts us: to receive Jesus that his love may brood over us, or to deny him to his heartbreak and our desolation." (Page 251, Vol. VIII)

I do not, in any way, wish to be destructively critical of the Church of Christ or of my own denomination which I have served forty-seven years as a minister. I write only out of a spirit of love and appreciation for all that the church has meant to me and the opportunity that my own denomination has given me to serve through the years. Mine is a "lover's quarrel", my only purpose being to try, in my humble way, to help correct some of the things which I perceive to be wrong with the church and hinder her progress.

In Chapter Two, I try to point out that there seems to be a conservative trend in religion today, as evidenced by the Moral Majority and the growth of conservative denominations as contrasted with the main-line churches which seem to be losing ground. Radio and TV preachers are affecting the influence of the major denominations. The problem is that their emphasis is usually on personal religion to the neglect of social issues except that, in some cases, they center on a single social issue, such as prayer in the schools. These words of Jesus seem to be apropos in this regard: "And he said to them, 'You have a fine way of rejecting the commandment of God in order to keep your tradition.'" (Mark 7:9) My major professor in Seminary had a habit, on the first day of class with a new group of freshmen, of shaking his finger under a young student's nose and asking rhetorically, "Where did you get your religion? From grandpa, that's where you got it! You have never had an idea of your own!" This illustrates the need for an open mind in religion, as well as in every other area.

The purpose of the Third Chapter on the ministry of the laity is to point out the fallacy of looking upon the pastor as one who is "paid to do the work of the church", so that the responsibility for the church's program is primarily his. This is contrary to the teaching of the New Testament. We are all ministers. The pastor is set aside as the leader of the congregation which is engaged in ministry. Dr. D. Elton Trueblood, a Quaker, is perhaps the leading proponent of this idea.

In the Fourth Chapter, we try to correct the misconception that everything that happens is the will of God. The Chapter deals with the Problem of Evil; in a word, why there is suffering by good people in a world that is ruled by a God who is good. The Chapter deals with human freedom, the idea that God has limited himself by the ends he has set. If his purpose is the making of men and the development of character, then we must be free creatures, not puppets.

The thesis of the Fifth Chapter is that Eternal Life is not just "life after death" but that it begins here and now, when one begins to follow our Lord and Savior, Jesus Christ. The chapter also deals with the idea that heaven would be "hell" for people who have no appreciation of spiritual values.

It seems to me, as we try to bring out in the Sixth Chapter, that compassion (or caring) is at the heart of the Christian Gospel. This lack of compassion which characterizes many pastors and is altogether too prevalent in our churches of various denominations is one of the greatest obstacles in carrying out the real mission of the church; that is, concern for the last, the lost, and the least. This, it seems to me, was central in the teaching of Jesus. *The Interpreter's Bible* (Page 289ff) commentary on I John, speaks of ways of loving God. The writer compares this to the human family, stating that everyone who loves the parent loves the child, so every Christian who is a child of God through faith loves his fellow Christians because he loves his Heavenly Father. Children in a Chinese village declined to accept needed medicines offered them by a government station; instead, they walked a longer distance to get them from a missionary. On being asked why, they replied, "The medicines are the same, but the hands are different."

The true mission of the church, Evangelism or "reaching out" to those who are outside the church, is the principal idea of the Seventh Chapter. Jesus said to his followers during his earthly ministry, "You shall be my witnesses in Jerusalem and in all Judea and Samaria and to the end of the earth" (Acts 1:8); in other words, taking the Gospel to men everywhere. We are reminded in Luke 10:1 how he sent out the seventy, two by two, to speak to people about the Gospel, the Good News of God in Christ.

One of the great hindrances to the Christian faith and the Mission of the church, as brought out in the Eighth Chapter, is the lack of Christian stewardship in the people of the churches. This means that we are not as aware as we should be that God is the giver and owner of all that we are and have and we are holding these things in trust, responsible to our Heavenly Father for the use that we make of them. This applies to our material possessions, our time, and our abilities, our whole lives. Our attitude toward Christian stewardship is illustrated by the humorous story of the man who was asked by a member of the Every Member Canvass Committee to contribute to the church budget. When the man said that he was not able to contribute, that he had too many other financial obligations, "Don't you feel that you owe a debt to God, too?", the committee member asked. "Yes, but he isn't pushing me as my other creditors are." The positive attitude toward Christian stewardship is revealed in Paul's writing to the church in Corinth, reminding them how the "Macedonian Churches, down to their last penny, produced a magnificent concern for other people." (II Cor. 8:1)

I once observed on the desk of an executive, a plaque on which were these words: "Please do not confuse me with the facts; my mind is already made up." In the Ninth Chapter on "Facts and Faith", my purpose is to point out the need for an open mind in religion as well as in every other area. It is pointed out, too, that one cannot take the tools that are used to deal with science over into the spiritual realm, to deal with spiritual values. There are, in effect, two worlds, the material or physical and the spiritual. Spiritual reality has priority over that which is material or physical. The important thing, however, is that one keep in mind that he needs to have a

4

mind open to new truth, in religion as well as in science. And it needs to be said that liberals, as well as conservatives, can have minds that are closed. When my minister son and I visited a church in Florida the Pastor's subject was "Practice What You Preach". His theme was that one should have an open mind to new truth. In the course of the sermon, he mentioned TV advertising for the George Burns film "Oh God". He said that he had not seen it and was not intending to, because he thought it was blasphemous. On the way out after the service as we shook hands with the pastor, my son introduced himself as a Pastor from Indiana and added: "Why don't you practice what you preach and go see 'Oh God' "? It seems to me that Paul's writing in some places lacks credibility; especially is this true of his attitude toward women, saying that women should be silent in church and that wives are to be subservient to their husbands. Those who believe that one part of the Scripture is as significant as every other part; that is, those who believe in the inerrancy of the Scripture remind me of the humorous story of the Irish boxer, somewhat of a ruffian, who was converted and felt called to preach. On one occasion, he came upon some of his former ruffian friends. One of them knocked him down. When he got up he was knocked down again. After that, he proceeded to subdue the group with his fists. One of them said, "I thought that your Jesus said to turn the other cheek." "Yes, he did", was the answer, "but he didn't give me any further instructions". This illustrates the literal interpretation of the Holy Writ, as contrasted with the intent.

There seems to be today a lack of respect for intellectuals, as is pointed out in Chapter Ten. One certainly cannot take all emotion out of religion. This brings to mind the story I read somewhere of a man in one of the more staid churches as he sat in the congregation one Sunday morning and began to shout, "Praise the Lord", "Hallelujah", and so on. One of the ushers came up to him and asked him to be quiet. "But, I've got religion", he replied. "Well", said the usher, "You didn't get it here." It may well be that we don't have enough emotion in our churches and our religion today, at least in the main-line denominations. Religion should be both emotionally satisfying and intellectually acceptable. Matthew, in his Gospel, quoting Isaiah, wrote:

> "This people honors me with their lips,
> But their heart is far from me,
> Teaching as doctrines the precepts of men."
>
> (Matt. 18:8, 9)

Yet, there seems to be a mood of anti-intellectualism today. This is illustrated by the common practice of referring to intellectuals as "eggheads" which is a term of derision. We are not to check our brains at the door of the church. It is brought out, too, in this chapter, that there is a trend in today's society to make light of people who try to do good, especially in trying to right the wrongs that are so prevalent in the present-day world. It is not necessary to go into it here, but there is abundant evidence in the New Testament, as well as in the Old Testament, especially the Prophets, that God's people are charged with the responsibility of doing all in our power to reform the evils of society.

In the final chapter entitled "The Devil Make Me Do It", sin and salvation are dealt with. Among other things, explained in greater detail in the Chapter, it is pointed out that we have a tendency to project our own shortcomings on other people or circumstances such as the shortcomings of the church, the pastor, or the members of the church whom we think of as "hyprocrites". This, then, gives us an out, an excuse for not taking part in the church's program. One of the ways of dealing with sin in the early church, called antinomianism, was used to indicate types of ethical thought in which hostility to the Law of Moses led to a tendency to immoral teaching or practice. In the New Testament, traces of this doctrine are found in Paul's writing because of his struggle to clarify the relationship between the Gospel and the Law. One of the sects which embraced this doctrine believes that nothing is sin except what a man believes to be sin. This chapter reveals various ways we tend to deal with or excuse our sins. The various theories of the atonement are dealt with and it is pointed out that the only hope for us is to be found in understanding the suffering love of God on Calvary's Cross.

II

STANDING ON THE PROMISES
AND
CLEANING UP THE PREMISES
(Personal and Social Religion)

The proponents of conservatism in religion emphasize what they call the "simple gospel" and are concerned almost entirely with keeping one's self "unspotted from the world". One must be "born again" and this is certainly in Jesus's teaching, but they are weak in their emphasis on correcting the social evils of our time or "cleaning up the premises". They are often preoccupied with saving their own souls or the Second Coming of our Lord, but they do not seem much concerned with doing anything about social injustice. They have the wrong conception of prophecy, based on a wrong interpretation of such books of the Scripture as Daniel and Revelation. The prophets of the Old Testament were primarily concerned with declaring the will of God to their own generation, not foretelling the future, except in the sense of declaring what would happen if people continued doing the things they were doing which the prophets perceived to be contrary to the will of God. We need, of course, to be concerned with both the roots and the fruits of religion, with this world as well as the next. So many are overly concerned with other worldly concerns, rather than with cleaning up the wrongs of this present world. There is too much time lost quarreling over labels, such as conservatism and liberalism. We need to be conservative in the sense of holding to that which is best from the past and we should be liberal in our attitude toward the truth; that is, one should be open to new truth in religion as well as in other areas. (I hasten to add that so-called liberals can be as closed-minded as the conservatives.)

Speaking of being open to new truth, we need to be aware that the Bible is an evolutionary book, in that it reveals the development of religious thought from "an eye for an eye" of the Old Testament to Jesus's "forgive your enemies" of the New Testament. Many modern day Fundamentalist Christians exclude every one who does not believe in the inerrancy of the Scriptures or the Virgin Birth. They are considered not only unChristian but sometimes are referred to as anti-Christ. We need to keep in mind the possibility that the divinity of Christ does not depend upon the manner of His birth. In other words, the Christmas story did not create His life, but His life created the Christmas story. Neither Jesus nor Paul ever alluded to the Virgin Birth and Matthew, in his Gospel, traces the lineage of Jesus to David through His father, Joseph.

Today, the "Moral Majority" presumes to speak for all true Christians on matters of religion and politics in spite of the traditional tendency on their part to say that Christians should not be involved in politics. They are often concerned with a single issue of their choosing such as abortion or prayer in the public schools. Norman Cousins, writing in the *Saturday Review,* speaks to this issue of true conservatism as opposed to the position of some who call themselves conservatives: "The term conservative has a specific background of meanings. It stands for the preservation of inherited conditions as opposed to drastic reform. These ideas are not only compatible with a free society; they have an essential place in it. True conservatism is opposed to liberalism but not destructive of it . . . they presume to speak in the name of Christianity, many of them, but they use it as though it were a blowtorch for consuming the Christian spirit" . . . Robert Taft, he says, was a genuine conservative . . . "there were few stronger voices on the issue of civil rights and racial equality . . . As it concerned the United Nations, an object of supreme contempt by those who now speak in his name, Senator Taft felt that what was needed was not weaker but stronger world organization . . . . In fact, this was the theme of his book on American foreign policy". Those in the liberal school of thought commonly think of the Hebrew prophets as progressives or liberals, blazing the trails of new moral ideals. There is, of course, something to that idea. But they never thought they were liberals. They thought they were conservatives trying to save a great tradition from being lost and were not consciously trying to gain something new.

We are today surrendering many of the old-fashioned moral ideals. One example is society's acceptance of men and women living together without the commitment of marriage and with the accompanying breakdown of family life. Are we not losing something good and basic in society when we lose the old-fashioned idea of a man and woman loving each other so much that they do not care to love anyone else and so building a permanent home that gives the children the strong security of parents who love each other "for better, for worse, until death us do part."? Such traditions do not enslave us. They liberate, release, enrich us. How strong a thing a great tradition can be. In Nazi Germany, other institutions, one after another, went down before Hitler. No other institutional voice ever dared to speak out against Nazi policies except the Church. Many were Lutherans whose tradition goes back to Martin Luther who once confronted an emperor and said of his action: "Here I stand, I can do no other; God help me. Amen." Contrast with this the present-day Lutherans of the Missouri Synod who are fighting in trenches long deserted by some of the best Christian scholarship, defending such untenable issues as the inerrancy of the Scriptures. The true Christian tradition doesn't enslave us; it releases and enriches us. How does one justify, on the basis of Martin Luther's theology to say nothing of the teaching of our Lord, the refusal of some Lutheran pastors to co-operate with pastors of other communions?

"In my Father's house are many rooms" said Jesus and "I go to prepare a place for you." (John 14:2) This is the promise of Jesus on which we as Christians stand. Without

10

this hope and this faith we would be of all men most miserable. Without it, this earthly existence does not make sense. It is all a cruel joke. It is our Lord who has given us the happy feeling that to turn to God is to be living the kind of life that is eternal. The destiny of man depends upon his nature. If he is a physical being and nothing more, then the grave is the end of it. On the other hand, if he is a spiritual being, then there is more to come after the death of the physical body. Sometimes, in religion, there has been too much emphasis on the life after death which has led to indifference concerning this world, a "pie in the sky" kind of religion. At the same time, it is important to know the ultimate destiny of man because, without personal immortality, this world does not make much sense. It seems, however, that today we are concerned more with the means of life than we are with the ends. A civilization equipped with the advances and benefits of technology without any clue as to what man is meant to do and to be is a kind of cosmic joke. Yet, even Charles Darwin exclaims: "If we consider the whole universe, the mind refuses to look at it as the outcome of chance." By this he is saying that the cosmic process is rational and that nothing rational ever comes by accident.

There are the world-affirming religions and there are the world-denying religions. Throughout the history of the Christian religion, there have been both of these elements. Today, we see the contrast between Christians who find their only hope in the return of Christ to bring history to an end and those who see in the application of Christian principles a way of advancement toward the Kingdom of God on earth. Actually, the Christian faith is neither world-affirming nor world-denying altogether. It is world-transforming. This is what I mean by cleaning up the premises. I have heard preachers and others, as all of us have, talk about this world as only a vestibule, an entrance way into the larger room called heaven. The classic reply to that idea is that since I am going to spend some time in the foyer, I am going to try to make it as pleasant as possible while I am here. God created the earth and said that it was good. The late William Temple,

Archbishop of Canterbury, spoke of the "sacramental universe" meaning that there is not really a dichotomy between the physical or material and the spiritual, that all is spiritual because it was created by God. We live in two worlds, but the spiritual has priority over the material because it alone is eternal. This has its implications, certainly, for conservation, anti-pollution efforts, cleaning up the premises, for all is sacred. And we are responsible to God for the use that we make of these things. We are stewards, holding in trust the blessings of this good earth. Furthermore, God is the Father of all men and all men are our brothers. So we have a responsibility for others — all sorts and conditions of men — black, white, yellow; rich and poor; learned and ignorant. Just compare the world before and the world after Christ, if you are tempted to believe that all a Christian has to do to be a Christian is to keep himself unspotted from the world. Where did the new code of sexual purity come from, a code that is all but forgotten today? Where did the new passion for social justice come from? Where did that new concern for the weak and the deformed and the aged and the poor come from? There was one world before and one after the coming of Jesus Christ into the world.

Eternal life, according to the teaching of Jesus, is knowledge of God, not just endless time. It is a quality of life into which we enter now — the kind of life which deserves to continue beyond this earthly existence. There are no limits to the possibilities of this kind of life, the spiritual life. A traveler in Switzerland said that, uncertain of his way, he asked a small boy by the roadside, where Kandersteg was. And received, so he said, the most significant answer that was ever given him: "I do not know, sir," said the boy, "where Kandersteg is, but there is the road to it." This illustrates the experience of man. The idea is beyond our sight. It is a goal that can never be located, because there is much of mystery in our religion and relationship to God. But always, in the development of character, we are conscious that we are on an endless road, not always smooth but with many chuckholes, so to speak, and we are aware that we are on the endless road that leads toward perfection. This belief in another world in the light of which this one finds its meaning does not mean that for the Christian faith the present world is of little value. "The earth is the Lord's and the fullness there of" (Ps. 24:1) and "the heavens are telling the glory of God and the firmament proclaims his handiwork". (Ps. 19:1)

The Incarnation means that God Himself has entered into this material world and that He is personally involved in human history. The Christian faith is just a lot of words unless it is understood as a summons to action. To put it simply: The Christian faith is commitment to Christ in whom we find the love of God and by whom we are enabled to love the Lord our God with all our heart, soul, mind, and strength, and to love our neighbors as ourselves. With that commitment we can stand on the promises and clean up the premises.

III

IS THERE A MINISTER IN THE HOUSE?
(The Ministry of the Laity)

Through the years, as I have served various churches as pastor, I have felt that too much has depended on the pastor. I have come increasingly to the conviction that Dr. Elton Trueblood is right in his idea that we are all ministers, that the pastor of the church is not to be on a pedestal, so to speak, but has been set apart as the leader of the parish. We are all responsible, all ministers. Dr. Alan Paton in one of his books has written that "there is only one kind of preaching that is of value and that is the preaching of anyone, however humble, who takes up his cross and, not in the spirit of condemnation but of love, takes up his cross and says 'follow me'." John Wesley most certainly discovered the secret of spiritual power, but he did not do what he was able to do without the help of lay persons as well as ordained ministers. The days of greatness in the history of Methodism, as well as some other communions, have been times of great lay activity. The Wesleys succeeded only after they began to organize the lay persons into class meetings. In charge of each class was a lay person. The days of lay participation have been the greatest days of the church. But lay persons are often guilty of failing to take their rightful places in the programs of the church. They are sometimes prone to project their failure to do their part on others — the Bishop or the Conference or the National or World Councils of Churches, instead of taking a good look at themselves. I am sure that they are not aware of the disastrous results of their destructive criticism as far as the effectiveness of the church is concerned. In one of the churches I served, I became so weary of hearing in Administrative Board meetings that we should be doing this and doing that — meaning the pastor should do them — that I

14

finally had to tell them that we had all the help we needed on the policy-making level, that what we needed most was people to do some work.

As one who has dedcated his life to the ministry, I have been sorely troubled by the negative attitude of so many of our lay people toward the church. It is too bad that we have to spend so much of our precious time and energy in defending the church. The Communists must be very happy that we are doing their job for them, tearing down the church, creating divisions among people. I firmly believe that we must oppose any organization or group that divides man from his brother, whether they are under the banner of Russia or China or whether they pose as true blue patriots, while spreading hate and suspicion in our own land. When we hear the church attacked in any situation, we cannot remain silent. There is much more danger to our church and our nation from our silence and non-involvement than from Communism. It is important, too, that we become informed on these matters so that we won't have to remain silent because we don't have the answers. "Sin today," said Dr. Margaret Mead, anthropologist, "is the sin of ignorance, where knowledge is available, of failing to seek for more knowledge now that we have the means of seeking it, or failing to believe that the truth shall make us free." She added that this is the sin that the Christian Church is in grievous danger of committing. Too many people today are talking about rights and too few about responsibilities. We talk glibly about the responsibilities of other people. There is one moral standard for the minister and another for the other people, they seem to believe. The employer believes that his employees should be more dedicated to their work, work harder for less pay. The worker believes that his employer should be more dedicated to the welfare of his employees. Artemus Ward expressed this mood facetiously when he remarked during the Civil War: "I have already given two cousins to the war, and I stand ready to sacrifice my wife's brother." We want other people to be more responsible, but we would like to make some reservations for ourselves. One can not help questioning the standards for membership, whether it has been too easy to become a member of the church. It has been said that the triumphs of communism, naziism, fascism, and other such groups (and one might even include the Moral Majority) have been made possible because of poorly disciplined, inadequately trained, uninformed, and faithless Christians.

Much has been said and written about the Supreme Court decision on prayer in the public schools. Much of the criticism directed toward church leaders who have agreed with the decision has arisen because of the misunderstanding of the meaning of real prayer. It should certainly be more than a recitation of a prepared prayer or even a voluntary period of silence. Is it not true that the responsibility for the religious education of our children belongs to the home and the church? But we want somone else to do it. When I was in an administrative position in the church, I heard people say: "We want a preacher who can work with our youth; they are the future of the church." It seems to me that we had better concentrate on the adults. There is no substitute for the Christian home in imparting the right sense of values to our children.

A religion with a cross at its center costs something. If we are giving what we should of our time, our abilities, our material possessions, we would not want to do anything that would diminish the influence and effectiveness of the church. We seem to want the comfort of religion without responding to its challenge. But we cannot have the comfort without taking up His cross daily and following after Him. Norman Cousins wrote: "If the church has failed, it is because it has failed to involve itself in the human situation." It has been said, rather facetiously, but with an element of truth, that life is a football game, with men fighting it out on the gridiron while the minister is in the grandstand explaining the game to the ladies. The world will not be saved by ministers or by preaching. Not on Sunday morning, unless the people who attend can be inspired to a daily witness. The world will not be saved in the churches. The real decisions are being made outside the churches, not on Sunday but on weekdays by lay persons where they work and play and bring up their children, in their homes. The principal failures of the world occur in these places, the domain of lay persons, in offices, schools, factories, homes, stores, and voting booths. The church has not failed. The failures are to be found where each of us spends most of his time.

We are all ministers. Jesus said: "You shall be my witnesses" (Acts 1:8). There are so many activities, such as reaching home-bound and new people in the community, which mean so much more to people when the lay person is the one who visits. The pastor is a professional and it is expected of him, because "he is paid to do it." But people are so very grateful when the church members call on them, because they do it only out of a concern for people.

Some time ago, I read in one of the syndicated columns by a writer on the subject of religion who told about a service club convention. They were ready to begin the meeting, but the minister who was to give the invocation didn't show up. The Master of Ceremonies called the people to attention and asked: "Is there a minister in the house?" After a long pause which indicated there was none there; or, if there was, he didn't want anyone to know it, a man stood up and said: "I am not a minister, but I am a Christian layman and I can offer a prayer." Of course, pastors are happy to represent the church on public occasions, but Christians are Christians, whether pastors or laymen. We are all ministers. The pastor is just another Christian who is set apart to lead a congregation. The old idea that needs to be overcome is that religion is reserved for the pastor and for just a certain area of our lives. There are many who seem to like this idea of compartmentalized religion or that it is something preachers have, because it is easier to be a spectator than it is to be a participant. They are free to criticize because they are only spectators. Early Christianity was, for the most part, a movement in which there was little, if any, distinction between clergy and laity.

Bishop Ralph Alton once made the statement, when he was Bishop of the Indiana area: "I think the church has been

17

and is going through a revolution. The major change in emphasis is a change from the church being a group of people to whom a clergyman provided service to a group of people in service to others. The role of the minister changes from that of a person who serves his congregation to a person who helps his congregation engage in service."

In this confused world, how does the individual Christian decide where to put to best use his abilities and other resources? And how to conduct his life? If our religion cannot help us in these decisions, then it is not the right religion.

Perhaps one reason the church is showing a decline in membership is that we have not made church membership meaningful. Perhaps we should concentrate on making Christians of the members we do have. Dr. Franklin H. Littell tells us that of the three great rediscoveries that characterize the theological developments of the last two generations, the third event was the rediscovery of the laity. His idea, like that of Dr. Elton Trueblood, was that when men turned to their Bibles to learn about the nature of the church, they found that in the New Testament all believing men and women are called to the Church's ministry "by reason of the ordination of their baptism." There are various gifts and stewardships of talent, but all are for the edification of the faithful and the building up of the church in her work. The function of the clergy is to equip the whole body of Christians in the "general ministry". For many centuries, "a good lay person" was silent, docile, and obedient as is still somewhat true in some communions, most notably certain Lutherans and Roman Catholics. The clergy, then, are in the position of command officers governing a company of privates, most of whom have neither the inclination nor the information to raise questions. The pastor is trained in monologue and there is no dialogue.

Those who think of the church as a live and well-disciplined people of God have a quite different view from those to whom the church is an institution run by trained professionals for a silent mass of spectators. The fact remains that the God of the Bible calls all who would honor Him to the narrow way of devotion and servanthood. Harvey Cox, in his book *The Secular City* points out the difficulty which the clergy person encounters when he attempts to become the Christian presence outside the church, in the secular world. He says: "The only way clergy can ever change the way in which the word they use is perceived is to refuse to play the role of antiquarian and medicine man in which society casts them. But this is difficult, because it is what they are paid for." The difficulty is that the pastor's witness is not as effective as the layman's, because what he says is what people expect him to say, by reason of his role as pastor. This can be illustrated by a parable from Kierkegaard. A traveling circus once broke into flames just after it had set up outside a Danish village. The manager turned to the performers who were already dressed for their acts and sent the clown to call the villagers to help put out the fire, which could not only destroy the circus but might spread through the dry fields and envelop the town itself. Dashing pell-mell to the village square, the painted clown shouted to everyone to come to the circus and help put out the fire. The villagers laughed and applauded this novel way of tricking them into coming to the big top. The clown wept and pleaded. He insisted that he was not putting on an act but that the town really was in mortal danger. The more he implored the more the villagers howled until the fire leaped across the fields and spread to the town itself. Before the villagers knew it, their homes had been destroyed. Thus, Cox reminds us that the problem of the clergy speaking today is that their role is such that what they say can be safely ignored, like the clown. Thus, the task is the lay person's at least to a great extent. But the pastor can no longer play the role of the "beloved pastor" or the "good Joe". Either he exerts influence for Jesus Christ or conforms to the popular desires of a congregation and fits into their mold. In other words, he has to be a prophet whose task is to inspire and to train the laypersons for their task. Bishop Frank said: "A vocal church, the church with a voice, means at least two things: maturity in the pulpit and responsibility in the pews. Protestant laypersons can silence the church by withdrawng financial support, by boycotting the pastor, by attacking the leadership of the church, its literature, its message. But such actions can be utterly irresponsible." Bishop Frank further said: "It is a great moment . . . to realize that the church, as Christ formed it yeas ago, was not a crowd watching a performance. But persons engaged in a ministry to other persons."

Dr. Elton Trueblood in his *The Future of the Christian* sets forth four relatively untapped potential human resources for the church: laymen, women, retired persons, and youth. This involvement of laity does not make the pastor less, but more important, for he should be in the position where he can inspire, train, and lead the lay people in the tasks of the church and community. But when the pastor and his staff do those jobs which lay people need to do, this indicates a sign of sickness in the church. And the program of the church suffers. As to the youth, most of our youth programs are set up to *serve* youth. "Youth must be served" was our slogan in my early days of the ministry and is even yet to a great extent. What young people really need is to be needed and to know that they are needed. The only way to attract youth is to bring them into the ministry of the church. The churches that are growing today are the ones in which the lay people are deeply involved in the church's ministry — not spectators, but members of the team.

Especially in these days of twisted values and violence and injustice and man's inhumanity to man, we need to work together, pastor and people, against these evils. And it cannot be done without committed lay people, unless we are members of the crew and not merely passengers. In order for the church to be faithful to her mission in these tragic days, we must have teamwork. As Paul said (Romans 12:4, 5): "For as in one body, we have many members, and all the members do not have the same function, so we, though many, are one body in Christ, and individually members one of the other." We are all ministers. A member of the body that no longer functions is not a member. Nor is a member of the church, who is able to be active and is not, really a member.

The job is not the pastor's alone, nor even the faithful few. Is there a minister in your house?

IV

TRANSFORMING TRAGEDY
(The Problem of Evil and Suffering)

One of the most prevalent misconceptions I have encountered throughout my ministry is the idea which people have that everything that happens is God's will. When a baby dies, from whatever cause, "God took him". When a man is killed in an accident, "his number was up". In one partish in particular where I served several years, I heard so many times from a funeral director who was a member of my church, especially when the deceased died in an accident, by suicide, or any unusual situation, that "the persons's time had come". Realizing full well that what I am about to state goes against what the "plan of salvation" people believe, I feel constrained to state that God never willed the death of anyone. I believe that Jesus went to the cross of his own volition, that it was not God's will that His Son should die on the cross, rather that men would follow Him. However, in the circumstances brought about by evil men, God preferred that Jesus go to the cross rather than run away. This does not mean that Jesus could not have run away. If God planned Jesus's crucifixion in the sense that Jesus had no choice, then He also planned that Judas betray Him. In that case, Judas had no choice. It follows, then, that Judas was not to blame. It seems to me to be blasphemy to say that everything that happens is God's will. So many people in the churches I have served have seemed to find comfort in believing that God "took" their loved one. Often, when the deceased was a little child, it was because God needed him for his "heavenly garden" or some other such illogical and repulsive reason.

This question which theologians refer to as "The Problem of Evil" has concerned the best minds through the generations. And it is only natural and human for us to ask, when a tragedy comes to us or a calamity comes to the world: "Why did God permit this to happen?" We do not have all the answers, but we do know that God has the power to transform tragedy and the individual has the ability to capitalize on calamity. It can make us better or bitter, depending on our reaction. As Dr. E. Stanley Jones has said, "when fate throws a dagger at us, we can catch it by the blade and let it cut us to the quick or we can catch it by the handle and use it as an instrument of defense". Dr. Harris Franklin Rall, in his book, *Christianity*, has written: "A world without pain would be one in which life would be impossible and out of suffering has come the noblest fruitage of human life".

What shall we do with these tragedies which come to us? Or to put it another way, what will they do to us? The answer is to be found in the cross of Christ. Jesus did not submit to the cross with resignation. He took hold of the situation and transformed it into a glorious victory. The Cross forever remains the symbol of the triumphant use of suffering to further the holy purposes of God. For that reason, I have long had the feeling that the crucifix rather than the cross, or as well as the cross, should have a prominent place in our churches. This does not mean in any way to minimize the significance of the resurrection. All the ways of God are not always clear to us. We do not always understand. But, because God is love, nothing can happen to us that is just meaningless torture. Because we do know God as He is revealed in Jesus, we know that though we don't have the answer, there is an answer and in that faith we can be content. Even Jesus did not say "I have explained the world". What He did say was, "I have overcome the world" (John 16:33)

It can be said that there are two sides to the Cross. On one side is God's judgment on the sin of man, the evil that would lead to the crucifixion of the only begotten Son of God. On the other side is the love of God in Christ, love so great that it would cause the dying Christ to say, "Father, forgive them; for they know not what they do." (Luke 23:34) A love so great that the Roman soldier could say: "Certainly this was a righteous man". (Luke 23:47 KJV) One cannot stand in the presence of the Cross and truly understand its meanng without having his life changed. For here is the supreme revelation of the love of our Heavenly Father. The Apostle Paul understood that so well that he felt himself as having been crucified with Christ. And he has told us: "Who shall separate us from the love of Christ? . . . For I am sure that neither death, nor life, nor angels, nor principalities, nor things present, nor things to come, nor powers, nor height, nor depth, nor anything else in all creation, will be able to separate us from the love of God in Christ Jesus our Lord." (Romans 8:35, 38)

The late Dr. Leslie Weatherhead, for many years pastor of the City Temple in London, has written a little book, *The Will of God* which I have found most helpful in explaining God's will in reference to the tragedies of life. He speaks of God's intentional will, His circumstantial will, and His ultimate will. As to the first, there is the will of God which has to do with His intention. For example, it was His intention that men would follow His Son, our Savior. As to His circumstantial will, he states that in the circumstances brought about by evil men, it was God's will that His Son submit to the cross rather than run away. And, as to His ultimate will, the tragedies which come to us can achieve good ends and further God's purposes if we react in the right way and use these things for the development of character and for the good of our world. Dr. Weatherhead has said that God's ultimate goal is the goal which He reaches not only in spite of all that man may do, but even using man's evil to further His own plans such as Jesus accepting death in such a positive way as to lead to God's ultimate will. We do not always react in this positive manner.

Wordsworth wrote:

"How oft in darkness and amid the many shapes of
joyless daylight, when the fretful stir
Unprofitable, and the fever of the world,
Have hung upon the beatings of my heart —

How oft, in spirit have I turned to thee (his beloved
river),
O sylvan Wye! Thou wanderer through the woods,
How often has my spirit turned to thee!"

"The fretful stir unprofitable" refers to the stresses of life
which harm us if we do not react to them in a positive way.
The stomach ulcer has been called "the wound stripe of
civilization". So much of modern life is conducive to ulcers,
high blood pressure, heart disease, and related ailments.
There is so much impatience, fruitless haste, anxious frustra-
tion. So much "fetful stir" is "unprofitable" because it
achieves no purpose.

Savonarola was a Roman Catholic who, in the Protestant
faith, might be termed an evangelist for he won over the city
of Florence and might have done so for all of Italy had it not
been for the Pope who tortured the saint until he at last died.
Just before he died, he said: "They may kill me, they may
tear me in pieces but never, never, never shall they tear from
my heart the living Christ." Jesus said to His disciples: "Be of
good cheer, I have overcome the world" (John 16:33).
Whenever we think of Him, we think of the word "triumph". In
spite of the fact that He died on the cross and was deserted
by His followers, we cannot think of Him without thinking of
victory and triumph in who He was and what He did. The
apostle Paul said confidently that he had learned in whatever
condition he found himself, he was content because of his
deep faith in God and the eventual triumph of righteousness.
The poet Tennyson in *Ulysses* speaks of being: "Made
weak by time and fate, but strong in will. To strive, to seek, to
find and not to yield."

In any consideration of the will of God, we cannot ignore
the question of unanswered prayer. How do we explain the
fact that some claim to have their prayers answered, while
others, just as devout, do not seem to have their prayers
answered? Sometimes, of course, we pray for trivial things or
things not worth calling upon God for, such as passing an
examination in school when we have not studied for it. We

recall the case of little Kathy Fiscus of California who fell into a narrow, open well. Many people worked to free her to no avail. Millions of people prayed for her rescue. When, finally, the rescuers reached her, she was dead. All across the nation many people wondered about the efficacy of prayer because of their disappointment that their petitions had not been answered. Actually, there is no such thing as unanswered prayer. We may not get what we want but our prayer is never unheeded. God knows our needs better than we know them. In His infinite wisdom, He can see further than we can see. And He has given us freedom — to fall into a well or to get pushed into a well, for example. We may pray for some cross we bear to be removed. Instead, we may receive the strength to bear our burden. When a minister stands by distraught parents who have lost a child in a tragic accident and they ask "Why has this happened to us?" The minister can only say "I do not know why, but we must trust in God who will give us the strength to bear this heavy burden which has been placed upon us." God never causes these tragedies; but He has given us freedom, as we have said previously. He could have made us puppets whose strings he would control, but He has chosen instead to make us free creatures with the possibility of suffering tragedy. He performs miracles, but He does not interfere with the natural order of the universe. When we do certain things or fail to do certain things, we get hurt. When we jump out of an airplane without a parachute, we get killed. But God has limited Himself by the ends He has set or the purpose He has for us, which is the making of men, the development of character. And this can only happen to men — not puppets. Since God has given us freedom, we can make wrong choices. And, though we may be forgiven, we still have to take the consequences. Whether our difficulty is the result of wrong choices or not, we can still react in such a positive way that it will be for our good. Phillips Brooks, one of America's greatest preachers, started out to be a teacher but he failed miserably, unable to maintain discipline. It was said that he had no control over the boys in his classes. But he did not let that defeat him. It taught him some things and he turned to the ministry, becoming, some feel, the greatest American preacher. He was a sweet-spirited man, "A power in the pulpit, a scholar." His early experiences gave him a humble spirit, a sense of dependence on God.

Sometimes, however, there just doesn't seem to be a solution. There is no answer to our problem. But God will give us the strength to endure the experience and make a creative adjustment to it. And we come through the experience stronger and better than we were before. Not only that, but we may be able to help others, to provide the inspiration for another person to react positively to his situation. And what may happen to us when we call upon our Heavenly Father for His help? Paul's "thorn in the flesh" illustrates this. Three times he prayed that he might be delivered from his physical affliction. The thorn remained but he was given so much divine strength and courage that his affliction no longer mattered. Which would have been the better example to Christians in succeeding years? Paul, freed from his affliction, or Paul, out of his physical burden, crying: "Three times I besought the Lord about this, that it should leave me, but he said to me, 'My grace is sufficient for you, for my power is made perfect in weakness.' I will all the more gladly boast of my weaknesses, that the power of Christ may rest upon me . . . for when I am weak, then I am strong". (II Cor. 10:8, 9, 10) Those who live in close relationship to God are not able to be defeated, whatever may come to them. All of us have known people who suffered intense mental or physical agony, whose lives were an inspiration to all who knew them. Furthermore, the difficulties and tragedies of life can increase our sympathetic understanding of the problems of others.

In dealing with the subject of prayer, we are naturally brought to a consideration of healing. Sometimes God heals a man directly when divine strength and the power of mind over body are needed but with no repeal of God's unchanging laws, only through means which work with God's laws, not against them. Most often, healing comes through the channels of medicine and nursing care. It is more than a little difficult for me to believe that a recent Miss America, who had at one time one leg two inches shorter than the other, had that leg grow, as she said, two inches instantaneously. Sometimes, God does not heal a person; no matter how devout and how great his faith. There have been faithless people who were healed and faithful ones who were not. We dare not question God in these situations or try to tell Him what we think He should do. There is an element of mystery which we cannot clear away, no matter how hard we try. Apparently, in the mind of Jesus there was something more important in life than health. When He could, he made men well. When He could not, he gave them the power to suffer heroically, to "capitalize on calamity" or transform tragedy for one's own highest good, for the blessing of others and to the glory of God.

People of every age have been faced with peril and times of crisis. Whatever good has been done in the world has often been done by people whom others might call neurotic, frustrated, nervous people who usually marched to a different drummer and did not fit in the usual mold, often alienated from friends and relatives. People who do not try to change things that are wrong in the world are not often bothered by stomach ulcers, because they are not concerned with social evils, things that are wrong in society. We should never want to be free from Wordsworth's "fretful stir unprofitable". There is too much that needs to be done in this world. There is too much injustice, too many places where a little concern might solve a lot of problems and ease a lot of heartaches. This concern is just another indication, as someone has said, that man has risen higher than the dog which sleeps by the fire. Some of our uneasiness comes from the fact that we are headed in the wrong direction. We have chosen the wrong road, the wrong goals. Inner resources alone are indestructible, the eternal values. Jesus told us not to be anxious about our lives, what we eat or what we drink, or about our clothing, "But seek first God's Kingdom and His righteousness, and all these things shall be yours as well". (Matt. 6:33) The pursuit of these material goals always leave us fretful and frustrated. They are dead-end streets, do not take us where God wants us to go. There would be less stress in the world if we had a greater faith in God and His providence. Events which appear as tragedies to us are often not tragedies at all, from the point of view of eternity. The loss of a battle does not necessarily mean the loss of a war. Man's judgment is not always God's judgment. Charles Dickens was a frail child. He could not play rough games with other children and spent many lonely hours with books, his only companions. We feel that his was a deprived childhood. But it is altogether possible that this contributed to the creative imagination which resulted in such works as *David Copperfield, A Christmas Carol, A Tale of Two Cities* and so on.

There is a power in the world which is not our own power, a will beyond our own. And God's victory in the world does not depend on us. We are not building God's Kingdom; after all, it is God's Kingdom. We can help or hinder the growth of the Kingdom. God is on His throne. He is our refuge and our strength. And "we will not fear though the earth should change; though the mountains shake in the heart of the sea." (Ps. 46:2) Let us not forget the word of Paul, even when the very foundations of our society are shaken and seem about to fall: "If we live, we live to the Lord and if we die, we die to the Lord; so then, whether we live or whether we die, we are the Lord's". (Romans 14:8)

Harriet Beecher Stowe sat through the long nights in her house on the campus of Lane Theological Seminary in Cincinnati, watching the struggles of a dying child. It was then that she began to think of the sorrows of slave mothers separated from their children. Her feelings for them caused her to have a desire to do something for them. This she did by writing *Uncle Tom's Cabin*. This had much to do with the eventual abolition of the institution of slavery in our country. We, too, can take life's sorrows and difficulties and transform them, with the help of God, to our good and the good of others, to the glory of God. The tragedy of the cross was transformed into a great victory, because in accepting the cross, Jesus, through his completely unselfish, sacrificial act, revealed to mankind the great love which God has for His children; and by revealing to us that, though the body may be destroyed, that which is spiritual is eternal and cannot be destroyed. In the same way, the difficulties which come into our lives can be transformed with the help of God. They can increase the love within our hearts, increase our sympathy for others, make us more keenly sensitive to human need, to the cries of distress throughout the world.

Some attempt to explain the evil force in the world by making God responsible for everything that happens; some prefer to believe in a dualism which holds that there are two forces battling with each other for control of men and society; namely, God and Satan. Satan, of course, is the evil force and is believed to be a personal being. Many people perhaps, in addition to the Fundamentalists, believe in a personal Devil. There is of course no denying that there is an evil force in the world. Christian Science, the modern form of an ancient heresy, denies the existence of evil. A leading theologian of a generation ago, Dr. Harris Franklin Rall, has stated that Christian Science shoves the Devil out the door and he comes back in through the window. They refer to this evil power as "Malicious Animal Magnetism." When I was in seminary, one of the instructors said that Christian Science is neither Christian nor Science. There is no denying, however, that there is a tendency toward evil in the hearts of men. Whatever we choose to call it, it is there and, though God is not responsible for it, He has chosen to limit Himself by giving man the freedom to choose between good and evil. Without that freedom, man would be a puppet with no possibility for the development of character.

Paul wote to the Philippian church from prison where he was awaiting trial: ". . . with full courage now as always Christ will be honored in my body whether by life or by death". (Phillippians 1:20) Our faith assures us, to paraphrase Paul, that all things do work together for good to those who love Him and that nothing whatever can separate us from the love of God which is in Christ Jesus our Lord, so we may say with the poet:

"I only know I cannot drift
Beyond His love and care."
    (Whittier, *The Eternal Gooness*)

V

WHEN HEAVEN IS HELL
(Eternal Life)

This description of heaven and hell will not meet with the approval of a great many people who prefer to believe in a heaven with pearly gates and a hell where the unsaved burn forever. First of all, it is my contention that heaven is not a place but a kind of life, quality of living, which deserves to be eternal. By the same token, neither is hell a place but rather a state of being or mind, of life lived apart from fellowship with God our heavenly Father. What earthly father would condemn his son or daughter to eternal punishment? Did not our Lord teach us that God is infinitely more loving and forgiving than any earthly father? Most convincing of all arguments against the common conception of hell is the idea that burning in an eternal fire serves no redemptive purpose. This is completely alien to the character of God as He is revealed in Jesus Christ. I believe that whatever state of being one is at the time of death determines whether he is in heaven or hell. Furthermore, one may be in one place or the other in the earthly life, depending upon whether one is living on a purely physical and material level or a committed spiritual (Christian) life.

There are, in a real sense, two worlds, the world of the flesh (physical) and the world of the spirit (spiritual). God is, of course, concerned with both worlds but the spiritual world is more important or significant than is the material or physical world. Eternal life, the kind of life or quality of living which deserves to continue, begins when one commits himself to Christ and lives in fellowship or communion with God. In this view of eternal life the resurrection or life after the death of the physical body is a spiritual resurrection, not physical. There is no further need for the physical body. Dr. Harry

Emerson Fosdick has written that the dependence of the spirit on the body is only a temporary dependence, in preparation for a future independence. He uses the illustration of the chicken and the egg. While in the egg, the chick embryo is dependent for sustenance on the contents of the egg; but, when it is hatched, it is no longer dependent.

In keeping with the character of God as revealed in our Lord is the conception that there is opportunity for future growth and development after the death of the physical body. Helen Keller, blind and deaf since early childhood, wrote: "I look forward to the world to come. I look forward to a world where all physical limitations will drop from me like shackles, where I shall again find my beloved teacher, and engage joyously in greater service then I have yet known". In his book, *The Great Divorce,* C.S. Lewis presents the interesting idea that one who has lived a purely physical existence, concerned only with material values, would not be happy in heaven. We, however, considering the character of God as we know Him through Christ believe that he would not leave us only to turn to dust. What of the resurrection of Jesus? Was that not a physical resurrection from the tomb where He had been placed three days earlier? Paul teaches us that the resurrection is spiritual, that there is a physical body and there is also a spiritual body. The fact that the two unnamed disciples on the road to Emmaus shortly after the tomb was found to be empty, did not recognize their Lord, leads us to believe that His body had been transformed to a spiritual presence. Is it not written that "flesh and blood cannot inherit the Kingdom of God?" (I Cor. 15:50)

Heaven would be hell if one's life has been given entirely to the satisfaction of physical desires and concern only with material values. Not that these things do not have their place in the scheme of things; but, as Christians, our primary concern is with the spiritual values. "The tomb", as Victor Hugo once reminded us, "is not a blind alley, but a thoroughfare; it closes on the twilight; it opens on the dawn". The life with which we are entrusted is given permanent meaning and eternal value by the victorious Christ. Our work does not end with the grave. It begins again the next morning. What proof is there that there is life after death? With Thomas we may ask, "Lord, we do not know where you are going; how can we know the way?" (John 14:6) "Jesus said to him 'I am the way, the truth, and the life; no one comes to the Father, but by me'." (John 14:6) This is the promise of Jesus upon which our faith depends. Without this hope and this faith we would be of all men most miserable. Without it, this earthly existence does not make sense. It is all a cruel joke. "Believe in God," said Jesus, "believe also in me" (John 14:1), in all that I have told you about God and man and life and sin and salvation and immortality. In effect, Christ is saying "I am not deserting you and I will not forget you. Where ever I may be, I will be thinking of you, preparing a place for you." "The main cause of Christ's coming", says Augustine, "was that men might know how much God loves them." When we believe in Him, we are convinced that, though death is a great adventure, there is a purpose for it, more life beyond it.

Shakespeare has expressed the brevity and insignificance of man's earthly life: "Life's but a walking shadow, a poor player, who struts and frets his hour upon the stage and then is seen no more." William Knox has expressed it in what was said to be one of Abraham Lincoln's favorite poems."

"Oh, why should the spirit of mortal be proud?
Like a swift fleeting meteor; a fast flying cloud,
A flash of the lightning, a break of the wave,
He passeth from life to his rest in the grave.
'Tis the wink of an eye; 'tis the draught of a breath
From the blossom of health to the paleness of death,
From the gilded saloon to the brier and the shroud;
O, why should the spirit of mortal he proud?"

What is the destiny of man? As we stated previously, it depends upon his nature. If he is a physical being and nothing more, then the grave is the end of it. But, if he is a spiritual as well as a physical being, then there is more to come after the death of the physical body. Sometimes, in

34

religion, there has been too much emphasis on the life after death. And this has led to an indifference, apathy, toward this world. "Heaven is my home," A "pie in the sky" kind of religion. But it is important to know the ultimate destiny of man; because, without personal immortality, this world doesn't make much sense. In all fairness, we must admit that there is no scientific proof for life after death, the work of Kubler-Ross and others notwithstanding. We must keep in mind, however, that we cannot take the tools of science and use them in investigating spiritual matters. There is a skepticism today, a distrust of philosophy and theology, of the values that you cannot touch or see with the physical eyes. One such skeptic describes the philosopher as a man in a dark cellar looking for a black cat that isn't there. And a theologian is one who claims to have found it! Our Christian faith in God tells us:

> "Thou madest man, he knows not why.
> He thinks he was not made to die;
> And thou hast made him; thou art just."
> (Alfred Lord Tennyson)

When I entered the ministry, my father who was a florist and nurseryman, always insisted that I should improve the parsonages which were only loaned to us, so to speak, by planting shrubbery, evergreens, and perennial flowers, keeping the weeds pulled and keeping up the lawn, in order to leave the parsonage better than we had found it. This, I think, illustrates what the Christian attitude toward life in this present world should be.

In times of stress especially, it is natural for people to place their hopes for the future in a divine intervention rather than in a process of human evolution toward the Kingdom of God. A religious leader has recently criticized the "Jesus movement" which we hear so much about today because it is based on a completely unChristian dualism; that is, everything depends on what God and His adversary, Satan, do. There is nothing for us to do except to engage in emotional orgies, disguised as the dedication of lives to

35

Christ, being born again. Of this we can be certain, many of us in today's world have been giving our lives to the wrong things. Thus, we are living in hell already, when we consider the selfishness, the greed, the lust, the lying, the material things we have made our gods, the lack of integrity in public and political life. This is why our world is filled with hungry, haunted people trying to find some kind of satisfying life in drugs, witchcraft, astrology, cultist religions, astronomy, or transcendental meditation. Do you think for a moment that you can ever find a better way of living with yourself, your neighbors, or with your God than the way which our Lord has clearly revealed to us in His life and death and risen ministry?

VI

THE DANGERS OF AN UNLISTED LIFE
(Compassion)

In a Peanuts cartoon by Charles Schultz, Charlie Brown complains to Lucy, who is offering psychiatric help for five cents, that trouble seems to follow him everywhere. "I can't seem to avoid it", he says, "no matter where I am, trouble seems to find me." Lucy answers: "What you need, Charlie Brown, is an unlisted life." That, of course, is what some people would like to have, an unlisted life. They just don't want to get involved. The social worker went to the door of a home in the slums. When the woman of the house came to the door, she said, "Me and my husband we don't take no interest in nothin'." Of course, it is rather difficult to live an unlisted life, as we are involved in mankind whether we want to be or not. Every Christian remembers Jesus's parable of the Final Judgment when he said that the sheep and the goats would be separated on the basis of what they had done or failed to do for "the least of these", those who are ill-fed and ill-clad, sick or in prison. Of these, he said: "As you did it to one of the least of these my brethren, you did it to me." (Matt. 25:40)

A former District Superintendent, under whom I served for six years, had retired and was in a church which I served in the late 50's and early 60's. I remember so well his telling me that he had gone back to a church, which he had served some years before, for a Homecoming observance. He said that one surprising experience which he encountered was that not one person mentioned any sermon he had preached (though he was an exceptionally gifted preacher) but that many people talked to him about how much he had meant to them during some crisis in their lives, because he *cared*. It is

37

interesting to note that the opposition to Jesus in His earthly ministry was from the so-called "good" people. He befriended such as the woman taken in adultery, Mary Magdalene, and countless others whom He could help and who were scorned by the self-righteous people who were so conscientious in observing the trappings of religion.

At the beginning of His ministry, Jesus went to the synagogue in Nazareth where he had been brought up. He opened the Scriptures to the Book of Isaiah and read: "The spirit of the Lord is upon me because He anointed me to preach good tidings to the poor: He has sent me to proclaim release to the captives, and recovering of sight to the blind; to set at liberty those who are oppressed, to proclaim the acceptable year of the Lord." (Luke 4:18, 19). "Today", He said, "this scripture has been fulfilled." (Luke 4:21) What was the reaction? Were they proud of the home-town boy? On the contrary. They drove Him out of town, to the brow of a hill, intending to throw Him over, but he walked away.

In John's Gospel we read the familiar words that "God so loved the world that He gave His only Son." (John 3:16) Not the Church, but the WORLD, though I believe that He does love the Church, especially when we remember the last, the lost, and the least. We have made progress in race relations, to mention only one social issue, and in the treatment of other minorities, though we have a long way to go, such as in the equal treatment of women. The Good Samaritan parable, from beginning to end, is a story of compassion, those who had it and those who lacked it. The government is doing today so much of what the church once did; that is, in the field of public welfare, ministering to the sick and infirm. We place our elderly parents in nursing homes and many times forget them; while, in former years they were welcomed into the homes of their children. In many cases, they lived a period of time with one son or daughter and then went to stay with another. And the grandchildren usually looked forward to the coming of grandma or grandpa to their homes.

Dr. William Barclay tells about a crippled and house-bound woman living in a Scottish city. She received a notice that she was to be evicted. She had no relatives. Her nearest neighbor was a bachelor in his 50's. "Don't worry," he said to her, "I will take care of you." He gave up his home and found two rooms in an attic. She had one room and he the other. He did her shopping for her. Yet, this man was a militant communist. Not that we are trying to defend communism, but it is in reality not what a man calls himself that matters but what he is. The man who helped the man in trouble on the Jericho road was a despised Samaritan. Jesus's only test of discipleship was one's attitude toward his fellow man. In Jesus's parable of the Final Judgment the judgment was made, not on the amount of Bible study or time spent in worship, as important as these things are to the Christian life, but on the basis of one's reaction to human need, whether we have fed the hungry, clothed the ill-clad, or visited those who were sick or in prison. William Eckhardt wrote: "The world is dying from lack of compassion. If there is a missing ingredient in life, it is compassion." Mother Teresa, the 1979 Nobel Prize winner for her work with the poor in India, told of the time she found a man sitting in the street. She said: "It was painful to look at him; he looked so rejected, so lonely, so heavy with sadness." After she took his hand, she said: "His face was different, there was joy, there was sunshine in his eyes. The tone of his heart had changed. He knew he was somebody to someone." To be somebody to someone is what compassion, caring, is all about. Wilberforce was able, at great personal sacrifice, to gain freedom for the slaves in the English territories. A pious lady once asked him, "is your soul saved?" His reply was significant: "Madam, I have been so busy trying to save others, that I have forgotten I have a soul to save." A man who concentrates on saving his own life and his own soul will lose them both. And one so concerned with an out-going concern for others that he forgets himself finds his life and his soul.

An English philosopher suggests that the best modern translation for the almost untranslatable Greek word in the 13th chapter of First Corinthians which has been translated as charity or love does not get the real meaning of the word. Charity may be philanthropy and not much more. Love can be over-sentimentalized. He suggests that it is better translated in this way; "If I speak with the tongues of men and of angels and *do not care,* I have become a sounding brass or a tinkling cymbal." When Von Hugel, the great philosopher, mystic and saint, was dying, his niece bent over her uncle because she could see his lips moving and could not catch what he said. She put her ear close against his mouth and heard this, the last words the great saint ever uttered: "Caring is everything; nothing matters but caring." "None of us lives to himself and one of us dies to himself." (Romans 14:7) The innkeeper's wife in Benet's "A Child Is Born" spoke this meaningful word: "Life is not lost by dying; it is lost moment by moment, day by dragging day, in a thousand uncaring ways." A minister friend, when he was leaving for another appointment asked me to say, in a word, what I thought was the greatest fault or inadequacy of the church and the ministry. I stated: "A lack of compassion". I could have added a word from the late, great Bishop Richard Raines with whom I had the privilege of serving on his cabinet, "A lack of compassion" for the "last, lost and least." As long as we are involved in life, we will feel pain; if not for our own suffering, we will, if we are the least bit sensitive, feel the suffering of others. The only way to avoid it is to build a wall around ourselves, to build up a hard shell of defense, to not become involved in the hurts of the world. This is not the way of God. He became involved in the human situation in a unique way in the sending of His Son to earth. Christ became involved and this led him to the Cross. We all know people who have built a shell around themselves. Some-times, one of their defensive actions is cutting other people down. Sometimes they crack jokes in the face of sorrow or tragedy. Often these are very sensitive people but they do not want other people to know it. They are afraid they will get hurt, so they have learned to use cynicism or forced gaiety as a defense. Human relationships bring pain. The poet Edna St. Vincent Millay was said to have "a vulnerable heart."

Vulnerable hearts suffer. And they suffer because they enter into the sorrows of other people.

I have a minister friend who has built up his defenses rather well. He often responds to tragic situations with a wise-crack. But on rare occasions his sensitivity comes through and you see him as he really is. One such time was at the funeral of an older minister friend who had two minister sons, also friends of ours. Before the service, my friend was making light-hearted, witty remarks, as if to say, "Things like this don't bother me." But, after the service, when we went to the home, one of the sons came out to greet us. When my "tough-guy" friend saw him, he broke down and cried. Still others, however, are not putting up a front — they really don't care. Life with Christ cannot be unlisted. Look at His concern for people, recorded in the Gospels, because His one all-compelling desire was to do His Father's will. Do you suppose Jesus "liked" everybody? I wonder. I do believe he loved everybody. And there is a difference. Think of his scathing rebuke of the Scribes and Pharisees; yet, he showed goodwill to all men and often, by so doing, called forth their best. To everyone else, Matthew was a crusty old tax gatherer, Zacchaeus a mean little money-lender. Neither of them was of any use to anyone. But deep down were the seeds of saintliness. And Matthew became the author of St. Matthew's gospel. It was the miracle of the Master's love that brought forth the hidden character. There was Mary Magdelene spurned by everyone except our Lord. He was fully aware of her faults but was able to get through all those faults to awaken the beautiful character that was inspired by His friendship. He saved men and women like that. It was just CARING. I think the message of Jesus for us today would be that we begin with the people nearest to us, our families and friends, our business associates, the people we regularly come into contact with. Everyone can begin there.

We cannot have the comfort of religion without accepting the challenge. Billy Graham has said that the American people are taking tranquilizers in place of God. This may be true, but it is also true that we often take God in place of the tranquilizer. Think of the comfort in the truth that God loves everybody. For if that is true, then every man is my brother. If it is true that God loves everybody, then how can we permit His people to live in slums, or consent to war or racial injustice? If we want the comfort of God's grace, then we must respond to His love for others, too.

Another thing that an unlisted life does is to resist change, because we do not want to become involved. So we try to preserve the status quo and resist any change in our world, even the injustices of our society. What is the mission of the church in times of great change? The church is not yet united sufficiently, nor Christian enough, to meet the challenge of these days. There is a strong tendency in the church to become conservative (in the worst sense) concerned only with its own preservation rather than to get out into the world where the deep-down needs are. Often the church is concerned only with tradition, clinging to old customs, sometimes even aligned with the forces of reaction, going through the motions of religion, observing the forms and neglecting the power of God that is available to us to change what is wrong in the world.

There is no such thing as an unlisted Christian life. Christ has not promised that it will be easy when we become involved in the problems of mankind and try to change the things that are wrong. But He has promised that He will not fail us nor forsake us. And He himself has set the example for us. Think of the friendships He made: the Zacchaeuses, the Mary Magdalenes, and the Peters, not in the way of those superior people who go about doing good and are so conscious of their own goodness; but so simply and without show because He loved them so and was not ashamed to call them brethren. Is it not symbolic that when at last He died it was between two thieves? The great preacher, Dr. Stewart, wrote: "All His life he had belonged to sinners; and in His death He was not divided from them. It was — it is — His chosen place." All His life, He was stretching out His hands and saying "Brother". If all the energies we now use for our own selfish purposes were spent in an effort to establish right relationships among men, we would find that there is enough for everybody, so that no one in the world would need to be hungry. Have you ever tried to get rid of your own problems by doing something for others? We cannot have the true joy of the Christian life, without sharing the suffering of our neighbors and our neighbors are any people, anywhere, whom we can help; without sharing His concern for the last, the lost, and the least. Jesus always connected the love of God with the love of men. It is easy for us, when things are going well for us personally, to put aside all thought of those underprivileged, disadvantaged men, women, and children for whom there is still "no room at the inn". But we must all one day face the One whose name we bear. We have no valid excuse for not knowing and for not doing, for the call to compassion is all around us. On Jesus's own authority, we will all eventually be judged by the compassion we have shown, or failed to show, to our fellow-men. Are you trying to live an unlisted life or are you enlisted on His side in His work of compassion?

Comedian Dick Gregory told about an incident from his boyhood that he remembered vividly. He had had a good day selling papers and shining shoes and went into a restaurant where he stuffed himself with chili, cheeseburgers, a soft drink and a piece of chocolate cake. As he was eating, an old wino came in and ordered twenty-six cents worth of food. When it was time to pay the check, he said he didn't have any money so the owner knocked him down with a bottle, watched him bleed a little, then began to kick him. Then young Dick Gregory said: "Leave him alone; I'll pay the twenty-six cents." The wino managed to get to his feet and, leaning on the counter, said: "Keep your twenty-six cents. You don't have to pay, not now. I just finished paying for it." He started out, then he put his hand on the boy's shoulder and with the venom in his voice replaced by sadness, said: "Thanks, Sonny, but it's too late now. Why didn't you pay it before?" Young Gregory realized that he had waited too long to help another man. He had avoided getting involved; he had shrugged something off as not his responsibility. He had

43

done the same thing thirty-eight people did in New York as a girl was being manhandled and murdered; he had done the same thing the concentration camp guards and minor bureaucrats in Hitler's Germany had done. If the church and Christian people don't become involved, who will?

On the positive side, in spite of the tragedy, the whole nation shuddered when two giant air-liners collided over New York some time ago. Everyone was killed outright except one youngster who lived a day or so. By a strange set of circumstances he had been thrown clear, landed in a snowbank deep enough to cushion his fall and was found almost immediately and rushed to a hospital. He was badly burned and did not have much of a chance of surviving, but as he was lying in the emergency room, he opened his eyes and looked into the face of a nurse. She was a stranger, of course, but in his childish directness and faith he said: "I go to Sunday School." Trying very hard to control her emotions she said: "Then you have come to the right place, because this is a Christian hospital." How great it is that you and I and every Christian everywhere have a part in an enterprise which tries always and succeeds, more than we realize, to be at the right place at the right time to help others. "But the Samaritan, as he journed, came to where he was; and when he saw him, he had compassion." (Luke 10:33)

Are we aware of what the needs of the world are? Are we aware of the poverty right here at home? We grumble about government interference in local affairs. But in many areas, if the church had done its job, what it is commissioned to do, it would not be necessary for the government to step in. However, it needs to be said that it has been the Christian religion that has inspired most all the welfare programs. Are we aware of the fact that, throughout the world, millions of people, millions of little children, go to bed hungry night after night? The churches, it must be said, are doing some things individually and collectively, through Church World Service, the National and World Councils of Churches, to help meet the needs. But it is not enough. So often we are concerned only with keeping our church building in repair and paying our

44

pastor to be our private chaplain that we are not concerned with the underprivileged in our own communities, let alone the starving millions in other parts of the world.

Dr. Irl G. Whitchurch in his book *An Enlightened Conscience,* wrote: . . . "the Christmas story says that the God of Jesus lives and works eternally against every thrust of brutality, in every agonizing cry of the weak and defenseless, in the patient protest of the victims of exploitation by human greed, in the faithful ministrations of the family circle, in the loyalties of all builders of a better world. That God is here, as Frank Mason North taught us to sing:

Where cross the crowded ways of life,
Where sound the cries of race and clan,
Above the noise of selfish strife,
We hear Thy voice, O Son of Man!

The haunts of wretchedness and need,
On shadowed thresholds dark with fears,
From paths where hide the lures of greed,
We catch the vision of thy tears.

* * * * * * * * * * * * * * *

The cup of water given for thee
Still holds the freshness of thy grace;
Yet long these multitudes to see
The sweet compassion of thy face.

O Master, from the mountainside,
Make haste to heal these hearts of pain;
Among these restless throngs abide,
O tread the city's streets again.

Till sons of men shall learn thy love
And follow where Thy feet have trod;
Till, glorious from Thy heaven above,
Shall come the city of our God!"

VII

REACH OUT OR PASS OUT
(Evangelism or Mission)

There is no authentic Christian faith without Evangelism or Mission. Though, in the mainline denominations, there is not the emphasis on the invitation to Christian discipleship in the worship service or "praying through" at an altar of prayer, we must not forget that reaching out to others is our main business. The church that does not reach out passes out. And it must not be left entirely to the pastor. We are all ministers and we are all evangelists or witnesses to our faith. Though we do not approve of the methods or message of some of the sects such as the Jehovah's Witnesses or Mormons, we can surely learn something from their dedication and their zeal. It has been said that the greatest days of the church were the days of the Missionaries, Monks, and Methodists. This is true, I believe, because these were times of great lay participation in the program of the church. How many there are who have been brought to Christ through the influence of some dedicated Christian, perhaps more than those who have been won by all the sermons ever preached. In a sociology class at Johns Hopkins many years ago, they made a study of the worst slum section of Baltimore. They had two hundred cards on young men marked "headed for jail". Twenty-five years later, a Sociology class found these cards and investigated each case. They discovered that only two of them were in jail. They wondered what the reason was. They investigated and found the answer in one person, "Aunt Hannah", a teacher in grade school. They heard the same story over and over. "I was headed for jail but Aunt Hannah got hold of me and started me in the right direction." We will never find the road to life until we learn how to help others along the way.

In the Book of Acts, we read these significant words: (4:13) "Now when they saw the boldness of Peter and John and perceived that they were uneducated, common men, they wondered; and they recognized that they had been with Jesus." There is something attractive and contagious about the dedicated Christian life. So many of us today owe what we are to the love and concern that have touched our lives through the faith of those dear to us. As we think of their devotion and service, their influence is not lost upon us. It is doubtful that many have been converted to Christianity by reason alone. It has its place, of course, but seeing lives changed by the Christian religion is much more convincing. Dr. Alexander McLaren used to tell of a man of great intellectual power whom he longed to win to Christ. So this great preacher who was a power in the pulpit preached a series of sermons designed to answer the questions that were troubling his friend. The man came eventually to Dr. McLaren and said that he had become a convinced Christian and wanted to join the church. "And which of my sermons was it that convinced you to become a Christian?" "Your sermons?" said the man. "It wasn't any of your sermons. The thing that set me to thinking was that a poor woman came out of your church beside me and stumbled on the steps. When I put out my hand to help her, she smiled and said 'Thank you' and then added, 'Do you love Jesus Christ, my blessed Savior? He means everything to me.' I thought about it and found I was on the wrong road. I still have many intellectual difficulties, but now He means everything to me, too." What a brief encounter! Yet, it no doubt resulted in changes in many lives through a kind of chain reaction.

As Christians, we are not just responsible for ourselves. We are involved in mankind. "Never send to know for whom the bell tolls; it tolls for thee." (John Donne) We cannot escape that involvement. When I look back over my own life and think of the people who influenced my life, they are, for the most part, humble people who lived quiet, simple lives; people who were not themselves aware of their influence, sometimes a relative, a grandmother or an uncle, sometimes

47

a neighbor or a friend; sometimes a Sunday School teacher; sometimes even someone who did not know that I was aware of his existence. The Christian often knows nothing of the effect of his life, for good or ill. Once when I was pastor in a county-seat town, I was invited by the Principal of the Elementary School to have lunch in the cafeteria of which he was justly proud. I went through the line with him, went to a table and ate my lunch. Later, a mother of one of the children who was in the school, told me that, at dinner that evening, when she asked her son, Rusty, to give the prayer of thanks, he refused. Asked why, he said: "Today at lunch, our pastor didn't ask the blessing." Of course, there was no opportunity for anything but a silent prayer, but the point is that we are not aware of the influence that we do have. There are people around us who may never get the Gospel at all, unless they get it through me, unless they get the Gospel according to me. This places on us a tremendous responsibility. Yet, it is a glorious privilege, too. There is no joy in the world like the joy of knowing that someone found God, or even came just a little closer to Him, through us. In the Scriptures it is reported that certain people, seeing Peter and John, "recognized that they had been with Jesus". (Acts 4:13) How wonderful it would be if people we know or some we don't even know could say of us in their hearts: "They have been with Jesus."

We must get out into the world if evangelism is to become meaningful. Without doubt, much of this strategy must involve the lay person. The minister cannot do it alone. We are all ministers. We are all evangelists. The churches that are growing today are the ones in which lay persons are deeply involved in the church's ministry. They are not merely spectators, but participants, members of the team. Robert E. Speer wrote: "Any man who has a religion is bound to do one of two things with it — change it or spread it. If it isn't true, he must give it up. If it is true, he must give it away." A very striking illustration is Jesus's sending out the seventy. (Luke 10:1 ff), the use of teams of two. Their success astounded even the participants. "The seventy returned with joy, saying, 'Lord, even the demons are subject to us in your name!' " (Luke 10:17) During my ministry, the most successful organized evangelistic efforts have been lay visitation, people going out two by two visiting prospective members. For some reason, laymen are more effective in this type of evangelism than are pastors; perhaps it is because they are not "paid" to do it. One of the great periods in the history of the Church was the days of the Methodists and the days of greatness in the story of Methodism have been times of great lay activity. This is not to minimize the tremendous impact of the field preaching of John Wesley and others. But as long as Wesley attempted his work alone, he failed. The Wesleys succeeded only after they began to organize the lay people in class meetings. In charge of each class was a lay person. We are all ministers. Jesus said: "You shall be my witnesses." (Acts 1:8) Our primary purpose is to evangelize. I don't mean that we are to ask everyone we see whether or not he is saved. Sometimes it is best to keep away from the subject of religion. Jesus asked Zacchaeus not "Are you saved?" Rather He asked him: "May I have dinner with you?" The minister cannot do it all by himself, any more than the Dean of the Medical School can treat all the sick. As we all know, he is responsible for educating medical students to become physicians who will treat the sick.

The New Testament Church was convinced that it served a risen Lord. To them, the assurance that the crucified Christ was now the risen Lord was the Good News that was the foundation of Evangelism. Ever since then, the meaning of the Resurrection is that Christ is alive and at work in history. Evangelism is the response of the church to the risen Lord who can become effective in the life of the individual Christian. In the words of Paul (Gal. 2:20): "I have been crucified with Christ; it is no longer I who live, but Christ who lives in me." Our evangelistic task is to proclaim the Good News that Christ can live in our lives and to reach out to others the Christ who lives in us.

Christian Education is an attempt to nurture the growth of

the life of Christ in the lives of those who are already Christian. So Evangelism and Education have essentially the same purpose; this is, to make Christ known, loved, and obeyed in the lives of people. Christ becomes embodied not only in the lives of individual Christians but also in the Christian fellowship. Christ calls us to life in community. This is where the so-called "Jesus people" fail. They are so often not geared into the life of the fellowship, the church, nor into any real purposeful activity. It has been said that "outside the church there is no salvation". The truth is in the fact that life in the Church is part of the salvation that God offers to man. If the Church is what it should be, it is the Body of Christ; and this is salvation. This does not mean, however, that belonging to a church alone is all that is necessary to salvation. The Church itself is part of the Good News of what God has done for man. This means that Evangelism is concerned with the winning of people into the Body of Christ.

Evangelism does not mean that one's only concern after His acceptance of Christ is to keep himself "unspotted from the world" and to go to Heaven when he dies. It is concerned, too, with the salvation of this world, with feeding the hungry for physical food as well as those who are hungry for spiritual food. Evangelism, as is true of all aspects of the Christian religion, is concerned with the Kingdom of God which is both present and coming in its fullest realization. The proper place for finding and serving Christ is wherever people are. One thing is certain. If we are to get people to listen to the Good News, we must reach out to people wherever they are — all sorts and conditions of people. In these complicated times in which we live where there is little that is stable and unchanging, we must be prepared to adapt and vary our approach to Evangelism, our Christian ministry.

In the Gospel of John there is a great deal of evidence that, in the first century, the Church was forced to adapt the Christian Gospel to a new cultural and social situation. As Jesus had said, "You have heard that it was said to the men of old, ... But I say unto you." (Matt. 5:21, 22) The Old Testament religion was no longer adequate for bringing the message of life in God to a Greek world. It may be that present methods of Evangelism have failed because we do not fully understand those people whom we are attempting to evangelize. When Phillip came across the Ethiopian Eunuch in the desert who was reading from Isaiah and indicated that he did not understand what he was reading, this gave Phillip the opportunity to talk to the man about the Good News of Jesus. Where did this hunger to know about the things of the spirit come from and why would he undertake a 1500 mile trip to find what he was seeking? Many times, during my ministry, in Visitation Evangelism programs, I have been very careful to point out to the visitors that, when they called upon the people they sought to win, God had been there before them.

There are only two ways to spread anything in which you are greatly interested and wish to share. One is to live it yourself. The other is to talk about it. Some years ago in the *Christian Century,* the late Halford Luccock quoted his mythical pastor of St. John's by the Gas Station: "Then there was the charge brought against the early Christians that they were the friend of sinners, like their Master. I told my people that most of them could enter a convincing 'not guilty' to that charge. I asked them how many sinners they had consorted with, except at a poker game or some such affair entirely non-evangelistic. They never get off their beat. They stick to it as if they were policemen, no new faces in the pews that they had brought there, no friendships that might yield converts." We do not advertise our faith, though I am not suggesting that we ask everyone we meet whether or not he is "saved." Leave that to the Jehovah's Witnesses and the Moonies, though we could learn something about zeal from them. We seem so shy about talking about our Christian faith to our children, let alone our friends, and never to strangers. We find all sorts of excuses. We say: "Let the preacher do it; that's his business". Yet, we know that this excuse will not hold water. Just because it is the "preacher's business", he will be less effective than your non-professional testimony. And that every real Christian is so enthusiastic about his Lord that he cannot help commending Him to others. We may feel unworthy and we should. This will cause us to take stock of ourselves and enhance our own Christian growth in the process. All we really need is the love for Christ and a love for people; share Christ's concern for the souls of men. People, everywhere, are looking for something more than they have. Perhaps it is a reaching out for God, though they may not be aware of what it is they want or need. If we have anything to give, now is the time to do it. Peter Marshall, speaking of Andrew who brought people, including his brother Peter, to Christ, writes: "So, the success of the whole business largely depends on Andrew, for Andrew was interested in people. And Andrew brought them to Christ. Only as the church today is interested in people and will bring them to Christ can the work go forward. The work that needs to be done today is the work that Andrew is best able to do. It is the work of the ordinary men and women in the church and Andrew is their patron saint". Many people outside the church seriously doubt, not without reason, that the church is truly a redemptive fellowship. They see too many of us who are smug, "holier than thou", complacent, dogmatic and self-centered, no different from people outside the church.

It seems to me that it is time for the church to give people an intellectually respectable, emotionally satisfying faith that leads to action against the evils in the world. Though a minister has written a book *Why Conservative Churches are Growing* (Dean Kelley), I for one, as well as the author am not willing for our church or any other of the main-line churches to imitate the conservative churches in their theology and an unenlightened appeal only to the emotions of people. I am not willing to give up an open-mindedness to new truth for the satisfaction of a made-to-order plan of salvation based on their unquestioning acceptance of every word of the Scriptures. And, in some cases, an exclusiveness which means that they cannot co-operate with other denominations in any ecumenical sense. Man's questions about the faith, the Gospel, the Christian life, must be faced and answered honestly. Many people today in this enlightened age, are unwilling to swallow the "pure, undistilled piffle" that is being promoted by some radio and TV preachers and others.

The church must support creative living rather than crush personality and individuality by trying to put everyone in the same mold, by accepting their "plan of salvation" that cannot be digested by anyone who does the least bit of thinking for himself. The church must not, I feel, even though we may be losing members, lure people into its membership by a cheap or a half-Gospel. Religion and its truths, being the very truths of God, must be thought of as worthy of the best men, the best minds, the best thought and as demanding as science or engineering or any other profession. This, of course, does not mean that we cannot let differences of opinion or interpretation keep denominations from co-operating, doing some things together.

I believe that people are longing for what the church has to offer, providing it is something really valid and genuinely relevant. They are waiting to hear the church offer what they really need and it must be a faith that is not insulting to the intellect, as so much contemporary preaching is, especially some of the popular radio and TV evangelists who have only a part of the Gospel and use gimmicks that are an insult to the intelligence of thoughtful people.

Whether or not we will succeed in bringing people to Christ depends upon the importance which the Christian faith has in our own lives. If it is of little consequence to us, we will give little effort to reach out and share it with others. It could be that the first thing each of us needs to do is to re-examine himself in the presence of God in order to make sure that his own faith is vital and relevant to today's world. The major responsibility falls upon all of us and unless something new and fresh happens to us, in our own Christian experience, we can expect little results from our efforts. As Louis Cassels, a syndicated writer of commentary on contemporary religion wrote: "It seems plain that churches can no longer sit back and wait for people to come to them; they are going to have to renew their acquaintance with some of the verbs as 'go', 'seek', and 'bring'."

It has been said that the greatest field of evangelism is within the membership of the church. We need to get closer to the source — to Jesus Christ. In some cases, it will mean a radical change in our sense of values. Transformation of life in accord with the spirit of Christ gives us a different attitude toward material things in order of priority as compared with the spiritual values. St. Jerome said: "It is ours to offer what we can. God's to supply what we cannot." God does His work through us. God is already at work in the world. But we are to go into the world for Him, to witness for Him. First, we must give our lives over to Him, then He can use us in His work. Social action, as important as it is, cannot take the place of evangelism in the sense of confrontation with Jesus Christ. To feed a man is necessary, but man does not live by bread alone. It is a mistake to try to change the environment without changing the man. The world needs to be changed, but man himself must first be transformed. We need to pray in the words of the saying, "Lord, reform the world, beginning with me".

VIII

ALL THAT A MAN HAS
(Stewardship of Life)

Stewardship is a basic philosophy of life, as much concerned about how one acquires his money as with how he spends it. Christian stewardship is a living principle. First of all, it holds the unqualified supremacy of spiritual over material values. All property derives its value from its contribution to the development of Christian character in all men. Human personality forms the only concrete embodiment of spiritual values; thus human personality is sacred. Christian stewardship is concerned with far more than material things; it is concerned with the use of time and abilities as well, for all of life comes from God and we are responsible to Him for what we do with it. The stewardship of all of life is extremely important in any discussion of the Christian faith or theology. The late Archbishop of Canterbury, William Temple, in his book *Nature, Man, and God,* speaks of the Sacramental Universe. All belongs to God, the natural world as well as the spiritual world, material as well as spiritual resources. All that we have, our time, our abilities, and our possessions, came from God and we are responsible to Him for the use we make of them. Transformation of life according to the spirit of Christ gives us a different attitude toward material things. For example, what one uses his money for is tremendously important. In all the programs for raising money, the important thing is not raising money but getting people to give. It is not so much what the money does for the institution that gets it, but what it does for the people who give it. One man said: "I do not understand it anymore than you do, but there is something about it that blesses us . . . . Those who give most, have most left . . . I believe that everyone who dries a tear will be spared the shedding of a thousand tears . . . I believe that every sacrifice we make will so enrich us in the future that our regret will be that we did not sacrifice the more." I have been told that there is an inscription on the statue of a philanthropist, in Denver I believe, which states: "All that a man has when he comes to die is what he has given away."

As to the giving of our money, as a part of our Christian stewardship, I would not wish us to emulate the legalism of the sects which make tithing a requirement for membership. On the other hand, we could do far more than we are doing. Instead of depending on dinners, bazaars, and other indirect means of raising money for the church, we would have no financial problems if we gave of our means as God has prospered us. In so many cases, God and His church gets only that which is left over after we have met our own needs and desires and there is usually nothing left over. If we are truly committed to Christ and His Church, we would give from the top of our income, not from what is left over after our own selfish wants are met. This does not mean, of course, that all our giving must be to the Church. There are many worthy causes which deserve our consideration and our support.

Jesus said (Matt. 10:39 RSV): "He who loses his life for my sake will find it." Far too many of us fit the description by Matthew Arnold in his *Rugby Chapel*:

"What is the course of the life of mortal men on the earth? Most men eddy about here and there — eat and drink, chatter and love and hate, gather and squander, are raised aloft, are hurled in the dust, striving blindly, achieving nothing; and then they die — perish; — and no one asks who or what they have been." It all adds up to waste of life and the resources of life. Of a child who died at birth it was said, "Too bad he died before he lived." The same thing might be said of some who died at eighty. In order to find life in its fullest sense, the abundant life available for all men, we need, first of all, to see ourselves as children of a loving Heavenly Father, created in His image. We need to see that in our possibilities we are just a little lower than God; that "it is He that made us, and we are His." (Psalm 100:02)

Dr. Goodspeed has freely translated Jesus' words in Luke 12:15 to read like this: "A man's life does not belong to him no matter how rich he is." Unless we make this simple discovery of God's ownership and our trusteeship of life, we can never find life in its fullest, most satisfying, creative sense. To find life, all that we have and are must be used to His glory, for the development of our highest selves, and in the best interest of mankind. One of the outstanding examples of the complete dedication of life was Dr. Albert Schweitzer. A physician, one of the world's greatest organists, a professor of philosophy, he gave his life to the black people in the African Congo. This same spirit is to be seen, too, in the lives of ordinary people. It has been my privilege to know some of them. There was a noble woman in one of the churches I served whose husband, a minister, contracted sleeping sickness in his first charge after seminary and became an invalid. By teaching in High School, cooking and cleaning in after school hours, waiting on her husband, she managed to keep a home and her husband with her, raising a fine son besides. Hers was a heroic life. The only time I ever saw her angry was when someone asked her why she didn't place her husband in a nursing home. "When I married him, it was for better or worse; in sickness and in health!" While others complained that they did not have time for church work, she always found the time to serve on the Official Board, to teach a class, and to do whatever she was called upon to do. She was absolutely happy, uncomplaining, an inspiration to all who knew her.

When one is dedicated to God and sees himself as a Christian steward, his concern for others will motivate everything he does. There is nothing more diabolical than the excuse, "What can one person do?" There is no measure of what he can do. Look at history to see what one man or woman can do: Paul, Luther, Wesley, Schweitzer, Carver, Jane Addams. Of course, we cannot all be like them but we can give to God that which we do have. One of the paradoxes of the Christian religion is that of losing life and finding it. Ours is a religion with a Cross at its center. In the

Cross was the love of God most clearly revealed. There is judgment in the Cross, and love, redemptive, sacrificial love. One cannot stand in the presence of the Cross and truly understand its meaning without having his life transformed. Here is the essence of Christian stewardship — the interest of God in man, His love for His highest creation, begun in the Creation and reaching its highest expression in Calvary. As He has loved us, so should we love Him and love one another. It is sacrificial love, love that costs. Without that, what we give has no real meaning. Without the giving of ourselves, it is not sacrificial but superficial. Not many of us are making any real sacrifices for the sake of the Gospel. We are not giving ourselves. We give a little time, a little money, a little service, sometimes grudgingly, and the major portion is for ourselves. In his second letter to the Corinthian church, Paul, speaking of the grace of God which had been shown in the churches of Macedonia in spite of persecution and poverty, states that "their abundance of joy and their extreme poverty have over-flowed in a wealth of liberality on their part," giving "beyond their means". He adds significantly that "first they gave themselves to the Lord". (II Cor. 8:2, 3, 5).

First must come the dedication of one's self to God, to live as He would have us live. Stewardship begins with man himself, when we give ourselves, heart, soul, mind, and strength, to Him. This is where it begins but it is not where it ends. From there, our stewardship goes out into all of life, into every area of our lives, in all our relationships. Where money is concerned, we will be responsible for the nine-tenths as well as the tenth, the tithe, how it is earned and how it is used. And our time. We will not say that only one day in seven belongs to God and that the other six are for ourselves to do with as we please. All my life belongs to God, all that I am, all that I have, all that I can do. This is the only way to the richest, fullest, most meaningful kind of life. Losing our lives in such a stewardship of service, we will find them. The Christian religion would not have gotten out of the first century if the followers of Christ then had been like most

58

of us are now. Sacrifices? Many of us won't go to church if the weather is too cold or too hot, in heated and air-conditioned cars, to sit in a comfortable building. Yet, we can go most anywhere else, sitting for hours at a football or basketball game. And present-day Christians find all kinds of excuses to justify their failure to help those who are in need. Consider how some of the small, conservative, so-called radical sects have grown. It is because they make demands on their members. Jesus said: "If any man would come after me, let him deny himself and take up his cross and follow me." (Matt. 16:24). We have played this down in favor of an easy, popular, aspirin-tablet kind of watered-down religion. Not many of us will be called upon to die for the cause of Christ, perhaps, but we are each one called upon to live for Him, to give our lives, all that we have and are, in His cause; and, by losing our lives in His service, we will find them.

God is the giver and owner of all that we are and have. So we are accountable to Him for the use we make of our material possessions, our time and our abilities. We seem to want an easy religion. We like entertaining preachers. There is a premium on the popular type preacher, the "Good Joe", the "back-slapper". But then there is really no such thing as popular religion or popular preaching. How popular were the prophets of the Old Testament, the first century Christians? There is no such thing as popular religion with a Cross at its center. Jesus never did promise an easy life to anyone. He asked us to follow Him. But He did tell some of them that they would have to give up family, friends, turn their backs on everything. "No one who puts his hand to the plow and looks back is fit for the Kingdom of God." (Luke 9:62) Someone has said that it doesn't take much of a man to be a Christian, but it takes all there is of him. "If any man would come after me, let him deny himself and take up your cross and follow me," (Matt. 16:24) He said. By the cross, He did not mean the petty annoyances that come to all of us. He meant sacrifice. To the rich, young ruler He said: "Go, sell what you possess and give to the poor and you will have treasure in heaven, and come follow me." (Matt. 19:21) Albert

Schweitzer, asked to name the greatest living person, said, "No one we know can properly be described as the greatest man alive. The greatest man in the world is some unknown person who lives only for other people." Jesus said something like that: "He who is greatest among you shall be your servant." (Matt. 23:11)

I once read a short story, titled *Combat Chaplain* by O.R. Fehrenbach, in which the young chaplain in combat, did not know what to do, did not know what to say to the critically wounded brought to the aid station. He stood by helplessly, vomiting. He talked over his problem with an older chaplain, a Roman Catholic priest. The priest quoted a Baptist chaplain who had asked him, in a similar situation, when he was a young, scared chaplain: "Would Christ's teaching mean so much to us if, in the end, He had not given Himself up to the Cross?" The next time, in combat, the young chaplain found himself; he walked into an exposed area to carry the wounded doctor back to the bunker and discovered that he did not need to say anything to the wounded and dying. Courage, like the Word of God, must be made flesh to have meaning. Without Christ's sacrifice, who would heed his words? At last the young chaplain knew why he was there — to help these men through the cruelest hours of their living and, if need be, to comfort their dying. He must walk unafraid through the valley of the shadow, in their sight, for only in that way was the Word of God made flesh. Only through his example could he give meaning to his words against the background of endless horror. And the Word must need be made flesh through us. There is no difference, really, between clergy and laity. We are all ministers. And God asks us for all that we have to give.

IX

FACTS AND FAITH
(Religion and Science)

I feel that in some ways the Society of Friends, the Quakers, are nearer to the heart of the Gospel than are some of the rest of us. For example, in their non-Sacramental approach to religion. As for water Baptism, I have come increasingly to the conviction that, though the ritualistic symbol may be meaningful to some, actually it means very little to many others. I do not recall reading anywhere that Jesus ever baptized anyone with water. Perhaps, the Quaker idea of the baptism of the Holy Spirit is much more meaningful. Furthermore, though the Sacrament of the Lord's Supper is meaningful to many, it seems to me that this Sacrament might be dispensed with, with little loss to the Church in general, if we do not personally find it meaningful. This is certainly not meant to criticize those who find it meaningful; but the Quaker non-sacramental approach to religion emphasizes the devout life of a very high standard and service to humanity, in a very real sense, through the American Friends Service Committee. Their stand on social issues, such as slavery, peace, and other issues, are closer to the heart of the Gospel than many other Christians.

The Quakers (Friends), an extremely devout group, seem to do very well without either of the Sacraments. It may seem paradoxical, in view of what I have just stated, about the simplicity of the Quaker faith, but the crucifix is far more significant to many of us than is the empty cross. The crucifix is meaningful because our Lord's sacrifice on the Cross is at the center of our faith. Paul said: (I Cor. 2:2) "For I decided to know nothing among you except Jesus Christ and him crucified." To me, there are two sides to the Cross of

61

Calvary; on the one side is revealed God's judgment on mankind, the evil in the hearts of men that would bring about the crucifixion of God's Son; on the other hand, the love of God is revealed in the Cross, a love so great that the dying Christ could ask God to forgive them who crucified him, a love so great that the Roman soldier standing by the cross could say, "Truly this was the Son of God." (Matt. 27:54) And today, one standing in the presence of the cross is moved to say the same thing, if he truly understands its significance. This is in no way meant to minimize the significance of the Resurrection. The following was quoted previously but I believe it bears repeating in this connection: Dr. Irl G. Whitchurch in his book *An Enlightened Conscience,* wrote: "Christians cannot too often be reminded that His life created the Christmas story; not the story, His life. The utterly transcendent reality of God's righteous spirit was verified in the moral integrity of His life." Dr. Whitchurch further stated: (pps. 88, 89, 195, 269) concerning morality, part of which I paraphrase and part I quote directly:

> As to morality, today morality is thought of as nothing but "a changing series of man-made agreements." "Justice is in the interest of the stronger; God is on the side of the strongest battalions; Morality is a front for economic interest in disguise; In the welfare of moral ideals morals follow the flag; honesty is the best policy; he profits most who serves best; treat the other fellow as you want to be treated, but do it first; life is bounded by the struggle for survival; morality means social welfare; the Golden Rule constitutes the final principle, the essence of all morality." (pps. 88, 89)

From the Christian point of view these positions reveal our atheism. This is a relativistic form of moral values, meaning that what is right and good is only the morals of any particular point in time. This denies that there are any absolutes in moral values; thus, there is no God.

   "To follow Jesus means far more than to work for a Christian reconstruction of society. But it does mean that. When a man enters the Kingdom of God he takes with him the whole of his interests and activities. His personal regeneration includes both a renewed spirit and an interest in a renovated world; he accepts with other Christians the obligation to work together to build an economic and social order most favorable to the growth of Christian character in all men; he believes that Christian justice demands the removal of all barriers to the abundant life in order that every person may face his own responsibility in respect to the claims of God upon his life, that what God wills we can do, and we must not evade His high calling . . . by his moral integrity Jesus of Nazareth translated the will of God into the language of human exprience". (p. 269)

The resurrection, or personal immortality, cannot be scientifically proved. It all comes down to faith, faith in a God of love who will not leave His highest creation in the dust. Our problem is that we are so conditioned in the physical senses that we do not know how to deal with spiritual reality. One thing is certain: we cannot take the tools of science, our methods of dealing with the physical or material world, over into the realm of the spirit and expect to come to the truth. When Jesus said: "I have overcome the world," (John 16:33), this demands faith, not scientific proof.

Tennyson has written:

"Thou wilt not leave us in the dust.
Thou madest man, he knows not why;
He thinks he was not made to die,
And Thou hast made Him, Thou art just."

Immanuel Kant said that the eternal law of justice demands a life beyond this one. In other words, he believes that a rational universe demands immortality. Robert Millikan, the physicist, looking back across a life's study of God's scientific law said: "The architect of the universe has not built a stairway that leads to nowhere." Edwin Markham wrote his own epitaph:

"Here now the dust of Edwin Markham lies
But lo, he is not here — He is afar
On life's errands under brighter skies."

John Wesley once said that we must "unite the two so long

disjoined, knowledge and vital piety." Knowledge is important, if for no other reason because what a man believes determines in large measure what he does.

There are fads in religion, such as Jehovah's Witnesses, Mormonism, the Unification Church, the Way, and Charismatic "religion" which has permeated not only Protestantism but Roman Catholicism as well. These fads have come into being because of the lack of vital piety in the main-line denominations. The hungry sheep look to us to be fed and if they do not find what they need from us, they will look elsewhere. This is why some other religions and pseudo-religions such as Zen Buddhism and other such beliefs are appealing to some people. Men and women can bear hardship, poverty, physical hunger and pain, but one thing they cannot bear very long is meaninglessness. Jesus's parable of the impossibility of the permanently empty house (Matt. 12:43-42) is perhaps more applicable to the modern situation than it has been at any time in the past: "When the unclean spirit has gone out of a man, he passes through waterless places seeking rest, but he finds none. Then he says, 'I will return to my house from which I came.' And when he comes he finds it empty, swept and put in order. Then he goes and brings with him seven other spirits more evil than himself, and they enter and dwell there; and the last state of that man becomes worse than the first. So shall it also be with this evil generation."

Some people today are so desperate for meaning in life that they turn to drugs in the form of alcohol or some other. They do not find what they are looking for, because hunger can lead to false answers, but a sense of need is a necessary condition of spiritual fulfillment. "Blessed are those who hunger and thirst for righteousness". (Matt. 5:6) This is where our brains come in. We cannot check them at the door of the church and find there what we need. Christianity won long ago, in an age strikingly like ours in many ways, because it could provide the only satisfying answer to spiritual emptiness. We can do it again with "the union of knowledge and vital piety". We need both facts and faith. Worship is not just for the purpose of making us feel good. It must lead to action. It is said that someone, unacquainted with the periods of silence in Quaker worship asked: "when does the service begin?" An elderly Quaker answered: "The service begins when the meeting ends." The great danger facing Christianity is not that it is likely to disappear, but that it will continue on a low level. This will be the case unless a more demanding kind of intellectually responsible faith wins out over the superficial kind of purely emotional religion that makes people "feel good." We must emphasize faith, intellectually acceptable faith, for people without a sound theology are bound to have a poor one. Theological questions are really unavoidable. Beliefs are important because they pretty much determine what we will do. An evangelist of a generation ago said that he was more interested in the Rock of Ages than he was in the ages of the rocks. Why can a man not be interested both in geology and the Christian faith? This is why we need a valid faith rather than one that is based only upon the word of the Roman Catholic Church (the Pope) or, as in Protestantism in some areas, only upon what the Bible says.

Belief involves not just abstract reasoning but the response of the whole person. An example is the question of whether or not God is. It is either true or false. If it is true, we should act upon it. You cannot just agree that He does exist and do nothing about it. Men cannot accept Christ and leave it at that. If He is telling the truth, we must follow Him. Those who reject the Theism of Judaism and Christianity as being indefensible logically are just failing to examine the best thinking of the Christian and Hebrew scholars of all ages. Many of our best thinkers could go along with the humble soul who says "I know God is, because He spoke to me this morning."

Our great need is for a renewal of Evangelical Christianity which is intellectually respectable and socially conscious. One of the great dangers we face today is the prevailing mood of acceptance of a vague sort of "faith in faith", the idea that it doesn't really matter what you believe, just so you

65

believe in something, even if it is faith in eventually winning a Reader's Digest or Publishers Clearing House contest. Do we really believe that the truth doesn't matter? This idea has led to a proliferation of the Christian faith into innumerable directions. An example is Joseph Smith's book of Mormon and the Jehovah's Witnesses' perversion of prophecy. I could name many. As has been said, "Everyone has a right to his opinion, but no one has a right to be wrong in his facts."

As parents and pastors we cannot shift the responsibility for the Christian education of our children from the home and the church to the public schools. We will just have to do a better job at home and in the church in giving our children and youth a valid faith. Our children and youth will not be attracted to Christ and the Church by rote recitations of "non-denominational" prayers which can reflect neither the words nor the spirit or teachings of any religion. The Church School teacher and parents, too, need knowledge of the Christian Faith. More than that, he or she needs to be a dedicated Christian, because, as we have heard so often, religion is not so much taught as "caught".

One cannot discuss faith without a consideration of the meaning of prayer, ". . . that Christ may dwell in your hearts through faith". (Eph. 3:17) As far as we know, there was only one thing that the disciples asked Jesus to teach them and that was how to pray. They saw that prayer meant so much in His life, that He would withdraw from the crowds and pray and that praying for Him was not a form, but the motivating power of His life, from His forty days in the wilderness to the Garden of Gethsemane. There are some brief observations that I would like to make about prayer. Most important of all in praying is the attitude that God's will, not ours, may be done. Too, prayer need not be eloquent. It is not directed to men, but to God. A rather humorous illustration of this wrong attitude toward prayer was when a reporter wrote, after President Eisenhower's prayer at his inauguration, that "it was well received". It needs to be said, too, that prayer is not for the purpose of informing God of

66

what is going on. As an instructor in Seminary told us, "always remember that God has read the morning paper." Another misconception about prayer is that it is a substitute for action on our part. Our religion has largely become a "cult of reassurance" in which Christianity becomes a mere vehicle on the road to worldly success. And faith a kind of super-aspirin that can be painlessly swallowed to provide fast, fast relief from the burning issues of our time. The Christian, following the example of our Lord, is to glorify God and do His will. I am reminded of the well-to-do farmer who always, when he said grace at the table, prayed for the poor, that the hungry might be fed. One evening after the usual prayer, his little boy said: "Dad, I wish I had your corn and wheat." "Why, son?" "Well, I would answer your prayer." We are not going to be heard for our much speaking. Sincerity is what counts. As the hymn says it, "Prayer is the soul's sincere desire, uttered or unexpressed." Nor is prayer, in any sense, magic. Its purpose is not to change God's mind or to bring Him around to our way of thinking. Prayer can be purely selfish. An example is the wheat farmer praying for clear weather so that he can harvest his crop and the orchardist, his neighbor, is praying for rain so that his fruit will develop.

The answers to our prayers are not always the answer we want. We tried to answer this question in the chapter on "Transforming Tragedy". G.K. Chesterton said: "If I were drowning I'd rather meet a burglar who could swim than a Bishop who couldn't." I fear the Bishop's prayer would not save him, though the burglar might. We have equated prayer with the search for a miracle, with our own lack of action and responsibility. Prayer is, for some of us, merely a means of getting what we want. With all the technological achievements and material blessings of today's world, most of us do not see the need to pray. Prayer is not a substitute for action, to be used only in emergencies. We must pray receptively, "Thy will be done," as all great souls have done. True prayer is not negative, but positive or affirmative; it doesn't dwell on our own selfish needs or desires, but stretches out a receptive hand to receive the infinite resources of the divine grace. Prayer is sharing one's life with God. As the hymn has it: "Work shall be prayer, if all be wrought as God would have it done". Jesus lived so close to God that He knew what God wanted Him to do at any time. Prayer is not much communication as it is communion, opening us to spiritual reality. We breathe without explaining breathing. We can pray without explaining prayer. It is the life shared with God. My son gave me a striking piece about prayer which he copied from the old cathedral at Coventry, in England. It is:

"Hallowed Be Thy Name"

"Hallowed be thy name
  In the home
    God be in my heart
    And in my loving

  In Industry
    God be in my hands
    And in my making

  In Commerce
    God be at my desk
    And in my trading

  In suffering
    God be in my pain
    And in my enduring

  In Education
    God be in my mind
    And in my growing

  In Government
    God be in my plans
    And in my deciding

  In the Arts
    God be in my senses
    And in my creating"

The Christian religion is a religion of faith and does not use the methods of science in dealing with spiritual reality. We do not see, in any literal sense, any of the great powers of the universe. No one ever saw love, only manifestations of love, yet love is the greatest power in the world. Only the individual's outer shell is visible. The real self with its ideas, purposes, memories, hopes, virtues, and love is invisible, yet it is this real inner self that is eternal.

We have been reading and hearing, in recent years, a great deal about the ancient Shroud of Turin which is believed by many to reveal the form of Christ and is believed to be the shroud in which He was buried. The form reveals a tall man with majestic countenance, hands crossed, imprints of nails through hands and feet; the right side of the chest pierced, lacerations from scourging on the back; and right shoulder chafed, a pronounced bruise on the cheek, chest cavity expanded as if from an agonized attempt to draw air into the lungs which occurs in crucifixion. The shroud has been studied and analyzed by scientists, including those of the Alamos Scientific Laboratory in New Mexico. But we need not depend on such scientific evidence for our faith in the risen Christ or our own immortality.

In his letter to the Colossians; Paul said: "Whatever your task, work heartily". (3:23a) William Barclay tells us that a close study of Paul's thinking about the Church lets us see that, for him, the Church is the company of men and women who have dedicated their lives to Christ, whose relationship to Christ is as close as that of husband and wife, whose relationship to each other is as firm as the stones within a building, and whose supreme glory is that they are the Body in whom Christ dwells and through which he acts upon the world. This, it seems to me, is "cleaning up the premises".

One of the discouraging facts in the history of Christianity is the irrelevance of so much that tries to pass for religion. And the failure of so many followers of Christ to understand what Christianity is or what Jesus came to do or what the whole thing is about. I am reminded of the story about the country boy who had never seen a circus. He saved his money and when the day came, he went to town just as the parade was passing. Thinking he had seen it all, he went up to the clown and gave him his money. He never did get into the main show in the big tent. In the same way, many of us never get into the main tent in religion. From the time when our Lord walked this earth and the Pharisees questioned His attitude toward the law, such as His approval of the disciples' plucking grain on the Sabbath and He said: "It was said to the men of old, but I say unto you . . . " (Matt. 5:21, 22), there have been people in the church who have not wanted it to be relevant to the contemporary situation. The Church is slow to move. If you do not believe that, try to change something such as relocating a church building as I have tried to do. If I may be personal, I have more than a few "lumps" in forty-odd years of trying to make changes. One of our greatest obstacles is people who live with their bodies in this day and their minds in another, facing the problems of today with the ideas and habits of yesterday. That was one of the things that hindered our Lord's purposes in the first century.

Try to change the thinking of one who believes in the inerrancy of the Scriptures. This is by no means an effort to denigrate the Word of God, but we need to keep in mind that the Scriptures were the work of men, divinely inspired though they most certainly were. We need to be open to the work of the scholars who have studied not only the Scriptural text, but the background against which the various sections of the Bible were finally written after having been handed down for generations by word of mouth. An uncritical study of the Scriptures is absurd. A Presbyterian minister friend of mine, unlike most Presbyterian pastors today, believed everything John Calvin ever wrote. I asked him one day how he could possibly believe in the doctrine of Double Predestination. His answer was that he didn't need to explain it, that to know that it is in the Scriptures is sufficient. Of course, much in the past should be cherished and preserved. But, when the Church is true to the mind of Christ, it does not lead to conservatism of the reactionary kind. You cannot place our Lord in this category. They killed Him because He was not.

A former vice-president of our country, seeking, he said, to explain what is happening to today's youth, said: "They are children dropped off by their parents at Sunday School to hear the 'modern' Gospel from a 'progressive' preacher,

70

more interested in fighting pollution than fighting evil, one of those pleasant clergy-men who lifts his sermons out of old newsletters from a National Council of Churches that has cast morality and theology aside as not relevant and set as its goal on earth the recognition of Red China and the preservation of the Florida alligator."

CBS's "Sixty Minutes" on TV recently engaged in a negative, rigged criticism of the National and World Councils of Churches, much of which was as untrue as that of the vice-president. A Reader's Digest article was on the same level. To me, the worst consequence of such slanted efforts to discredit the Councils are that they are believed by many people from the member churches. Some seem not only willing but eager to believe this sort of misrepresentation. One is reminded of the heyday of the John Birch Society which had the same result. The vice-president refers to the "modern" gospel. The dictionary defines the word as "relating to the present." The Gospel should certainly relate to the present, should it not? And as to the "progressive" preacher, I hope I can be included in that category. The definitions of that word are "a journeying forward", "a gradual betterment" and "onward movement". To stand still invites stagnation. Fighting pollution? The destruction of God's world would seem to me to be evil. As to the National Council, I am unaware that they have cast morality and theology aside. And the goals were certainly misrepresented, as they have been by many critics of social change. If he thinks we should not be talking about foreign politics, he had better get rid of much that the Old Testament prophets had to say. And as for the preservation of the Florida alligator, isn't there something in Genesis about God's creating the creatures of the earth and His calling them good? The prophets of the Old Testament strongly protested the actions of their government. And from the beginning Christians believed that their allegiance to God came before their allegiance to the state. Dissent and protest have played a great part in American history. Thomas N. Clark, professor of History at Indiana University wrote: "The concept of 'my country, right or wrong', may sound good in an elementary textbook or at a patriotic gathering, but people who say it never stop to think what it means. The Bill of Rights and the Constitution frown on this kind of indiscriminate statement. How would you ever exercise any influence on the government if you always believed your country to be right? That's what the vote is all about."

In the Old Testament, the "eye for an eye" idea of justice was practiced. But Jesus said "You have heard that it was said; "You shall love your neighbor and hate your enemy: But I say to you love your enemies and pray for those who persecute you." (Matt. 5:43, 44) How do we reconcile these two ideas? What of the differences between religious groups? Which are we to believe? The Roman Catholic Mass or the silent meetings of the Friends? Whatever we find most meaningful to us individually seems to me to be the answer, so long as it is intellectually acceptable. The tragedy of the conservative temperament of the reactionary kind is that it finds difficulty in recognizing the reality and beauty and power of a real religion when it turns up in new forms with fresh methods of expression, when it is able to stand the test of truth. If you feel by this time that I have been too hard on the conservatives, I hasten to add again that liberals can be just as closed-minded as any conservative. Only men and women who know what vital religion is can be reformed. And it seems to me that this has to come from the "grass roots", not by handing down in a connectional church, a ready-made program or even by bringing in an expert on "spirituality" (whatever that is) from outside.

In the great social upheaval of our time, men everywhere are yearning for dignity, for respect, for a better kind of life. This is what Edmund Burke called the "fierce spirit of liberty". This spirit has always been at the heart of our Hebrew-Christian faith. Why does the Ku Klux Klan burn churches? Because out of the churches comes the fierce spirit of liberty. Some have said that we in America do not have a national philosophy. Yet, no country was ever founded on deeper religious convictions. And we have not

72

lost it, though we may have forgotten its source in our Christian faith. We cannot have the good world God wants and we want without being the kind of people God wants, "for the living of these days". Personal religion alone will not do. Social religion without its roots in the Christian faith will not do. My son closed a sermon on somewhat the same subject by saying: "We might walk with our Lord in the stillness of the Garden, but He also calls to us to go with Him where cross the crowded ways of life."

X

"EGG-HEADS AND DO-GOODERS"
(Intellectually Sound and Socially Conscious Religion)

In these days of let-down in morality, as well as a dangerous trend toward conservatism in religion and politics, (that is, conservatism in the worst sense of that word) we need not only to have warm hearts but clear heads as well. In this day and time when intellectuals are called egg-heads and those concerned with doing something about the evils of our society, referred to as do-gooders, we are in desperate need of clear thinking as well as a deeper commitment, a more complete dedication to the values taught and exemplified by our Lord and Savior. As for me, I can find Him and know who He is in the Roman Catholic mass, in a Quaker service of silence, or in a worship service in any of the main-line denominations. As Albert Schweitzer wrote: "He comes to us as one unknown, without a name, as of old, by the lakeside He came to those men who knew Him not. He speaks to us the same word: 'Follow thou me.' And sets us to the tasks which He has to fulfill for our time. He commands. And to those who obey Him, whether they be wise or simple, He will reveal Himself in the toils, the conflicts, the sufferings which they shall pass through in His fellowship, and as an ineffable mystery, they shall learn in their own experience who He is." I must admit that I am not able to worship in the emotional orgies and excesses of some Pentecostals and Charismatics which seem to me to be an end in themselves and do not lead to any kind of action against the evils of our day. In my early ministry, I "cut my eye-teeth", so to speak, on that kind of religion and I found that many of these people were as vindictive and cruel as most anyone outside the church. If I had let them, they could have caused me to quit the ministry before I really started. I got absolutely no encouragement from these people; on the contrary, they did all that they could, including a trip to the District Superintendent, to keep me from coming to their charge as pastor. All this because I preached from a manuscript which meant, to them, that I was not called to preach! This sort of attitude is not confined to the lay people, but to some pastors as well. Some of these self-styled preachers seem to think everyone who doesn't agree with their anti-intellectual approach to theology is anti-Christ, if he is a leader of the Church, or headed for Hell if he is an ordinary person. Some of these preachers are, it seems to me, only a notch or two above Jim Jones of Jonestown.

"Egg-head" is a term of derision for intellectuals, but it seems to me that we need all of them we can get. Jesus said: "Love God with all your, . . . mind" (Matt. 22:37), as well as heart, soul, and strength. God gave us our minds and intended for us to use them. I am not thinking of the kind of intellectual who seems to be out of touch with reality, living in an ivory tower from which he never comes down into the real world.

And when I think of "do-gooders", I am thinking of people who refuse to accept things as they are, things that are wrong in their communities and the world, and who do something to change conditions. I am not thinking of the blue-nosed reformer, the stuffed shirt, kill-joy kind.

Our Bible, both the Old and New Testaments gave us the two great commandments: "You Shall love the Lord your God with all your heart, and with all your soul, and with all your mind; . . . . You shall love your neighbor as yourself." (Matt. 22:37, 39) There is a general mood of anti-intellectualism today, as evidenced by the new-found power of the so-called New Right or the Moral Majority. Some years ago, I heard a humorous story, told by a Bishop, concerning a sermon he heard down in the mountains of Kentucky which had as its theme the idea that education is the greatest enemy of religion. When a minister was called upon to give the benediction, he prayed: "O Lord, make us more ignorant". The Bishop said that he thought this was one prayer the Lord couldn't answer. The real accomplishments have been made by those who have dared to ask questions. There was that Frenchman who was almost beaten to death by his neighbors for practicing witchcraft. He claimed to have learned something new about disease and death. New? Ridiculous! Everything was known in the system they had. "The Lord gave and the Lord took away." That was all they needed to know. Change the system? No! Throw Louis Pasteur out. Just think of the contribution this man made to human health. The distrust of "egg-heads" is because the intellectuals are not content to leave things as they are in the realm of thought. We comfortable middle-class people who watch football on TV on Sunday afternoon don't like to have our religion or our economic system or our "keep the Negro in his place" philosophy questioned. Yet the real progress of the world has been made by the thinkers. We do not all have the same abilities, nor the same mental capacity. But we are to make the best possible use of the minds God has given us. Mental capacities differ, but we are not, as children of God, to misuse them or neglect them. They can be misused by cluttering them with filthy reading or by developing new and bigger bombs capable of destroying civilization.

"And you will know the truth, and the truth will make you free." (Matt. 8:32) As long as men are free to think and give expression to noble ideas, we need have no fear for the future. When you seek to know the truth and live by the truth, you will be free from bondage to tradition, prejudice, super-stition, sin. We are certainly not advocating that we throw everything from the past overboard. Our faith is rooted in the past. Yet, Grandpa was a sincere Christian but saw nothing wrong with human slavery. Then, men came along whose minds were open to truth who saw that it was wrong. We are going through the same process with segregation and other social evils. A college professor, naming the books that have changed America, listed such books as Thomas Paine's *Common Sense* and Harriet Beecher Stowe's *Uncle Tom's Cabin.* What do they have in common? Each of these books is a call to change existing conditions. Paine's thesis was a revolt against English tyranny; Mrs. Stowe's was a protest against human slavery. When they were published, there were those who were prejudiced, selfish, with closed minds, who would have burned them.

Sometimes we make the mistake of thinking we are right and everyone else is wrong. It is difficult to do anything with a closed mind. I am reminded of an elderly gentleman who, with a group of tourists was following a guide through the U.S. Naval Observatory. The guide said: "Think of it, folks, this clock is the one from which the whole country gets its time." The old gentleman took a batteed Ingersoll out of his pocket, looked at it and then at the clock and whispered to his wife: "Durn fine clock, but it's five minutes slow." Here is a remark of Bernard Shaw about a recruit to the Fabian Society in its early days. Shaw said, with deep feeling: "Good old Jones! His heart is with us. I wish we had his head!" Of course, the heart is important. But this many times is not the real problem.

"You shall love your neighbor as yourself", commanded our Lord. (Matt. 22:39) The do-gooder is, also, one who is generally looked down upon today. Some think of the do-gooder as a kind of prude who doesn't want to enjoy life and doesn't want anyone else to be happy, either. Of course, there are people like this. But I like to think of the do-gooder as one who refuses to just accept things that are wrong without doing something to change them, such men as Moses, Jesus, Luther, Wesley, Gandhi, Lincoln, Schweitzer, and Martin Luther King. All the progress throughout history has been made by men and women who used all their powers to shape events, to correct injustice, to destroy the evils of society, to make a better world. And we don't have to be Lincolns and Schweitzers and Kings to do that. The very fact of what others have contributed to our lives and education means that we have an obligation to others. We are obligated to God who gave us our mind, muscle, and abilities, and are obligated to our neighbors. And our neighbor is anyone, anywhere, whom we can help. Why be a do-gooder? Because we are not individuals living in isolation from others. As John Donne wrote in the 17th century,

"Every man is a piece of a continent, a part of the main . . . I am involved in mankind." We are to be concerned not only with the salvation of our own souls, to get ourselves into heaven, though there is nothing particularly wrong with the desire to get to heaven. But there is no particular virtue in it, either, if it is our primary goal. It has been said that many people want to go to heaven for the same reason they want to go to Florida — the climate is good and their kinfolk are there. Religion can be made attractive from a selfish point of view. People will follow most any preacher or any church that will promise health, happiness, or heaven. But we are responsible for our brothers, whatever or wherever they are. And if they are victims of prejudice or persecuton, we must do something about it. If they are living in poverty, we are to help them. If we want a brotherly world, we must be brothers. One of the real weaknesses of reactionary conservatism in a world that demands more concern for matters of race, poverty, and so on, is this lopsidedness, the idea that one is a Christian when he gets converted just far enough to be saved from his vices, not far enough to change his attitude about race and poverty and war.

Here is a true story of a lady whom some would call a do-gooder. In California, there was a Negro boy who was earning his money to go to college by working in a service station. Some people objected to being serviced by a Negro and threatened to take their business elsewhere. So the employer decided, reluctantly, to let the young man go. I suppose there were a great many people in the community who said: "Isn't it too bad? Somebody ought to do something about it." But one lady who had no responsibility at all for the situation decided that there was something she could do. She went to the employer and asked: "How many customers do you think you would lose if you keep this man?" "Oh, I suppose 18 or 20." She said, "If I get you 20 new customers, will you keep him?" "I guess I would." She did better. She got 25 new customers. Now, here was a "do-gooder" who did some creative thinking and dared to be a pioneer. To be that kind of person often takes courage, to stand up for what you know to be right, no matter how unpopular the decision. In *Inherit the Wind,* Clarence Darrow says to the young school teacher, Scopes, in the famous evolution trial in Tennessee: "It takes courage to stand up when everyone else is sitting down." Lord Shaftesbury of England, a great man of service, was headed for a brilliant career in Parliament, but the faces of England's poor haunted him, so he turned his back on his political career and devoted his life to those in need. When he died, all England mourned. Jane Addams of Hull House, Chicago, was from a wealthy home. She had convictions as to her obligations to the unfortunate people of Chicago. She gave herself to them. On the other hand, almost every glaring failure in history proves that selfishness destroys the very essence of life: self-interest, self-exaltation, self-gratification, all bring eventual defeat. Examples are Napoleon, Benedict Arnold, Aaron Burr, Mussolini, Hitler, and many, many others.

An ancient poet wrote:

"I sought my soul, but my soul I could not see,
I sought my God, But my God eluded me;
I sought my brother, and I found all three —
My soul, My God, and all humanity."

I still believe that it is a great time to be alive. What a challenge for us to do what we can to change the things that are wrong. We need to use our God-given minds, our abilities, and our energies to their greatest extent and dedicate all that we are and all that we have to the making of a better world for our children and grandchildren.Both clear thinking and a keen moral sense are most necessary if we are to meet the challenge of this day. This is the deeper kind of patriotism we need today, not so much the flat-waving kind. We are not doing so well in selling Democracy abroad. We are the best salesmen in the world, but are not selling our most important product. There are several reasons for that. One is, perhaps, that we are not practicing it too well at home. We keep feeding communism what to them is good news about bad Democracy. Another reason is that we are just not putting our hearts into it as the Soviets do in selling their ideology. They enlist their best and most talented people to sell their false ideas. We waste most of ours selling soap, proving that one cigarette is milder than others, that one beer has fewer calories and better taste than other brands. If we could get hold of it again, this dream of the unity of man, this passion for liberty, this sense of responsibility, under God, we could rediscover our moral strength and understand that we have more than a dream to offer the oppressed people of the world far better than anything offered by the Kremlin.

One of our bishops took his little daughter to see the Statue of Liberty. She was awed by the sight and size of it and looked with wonder at the great arm holding up the torch. That night she was restless and could not sleep. Her mother went in to her. "What's the matter, Josephine?" The daughter said, "I keep thinking of the lady with the lamp. Don't you think somebody ought to help her hold it up?" That is what all of us need to do. We must remember our beginnings, what we started out to do, really appreciate our heritage and, with a sense of responsbility under God, do all that we can to keep our minds open to new truth and to do all that we can to do away with the evils of our Society. There is a mood of anti-intellectualism today that has even permeated some of our seminaries where ministers are trained. In these days of the Jesus freaks and bumper stickers suggesting that you "honk if you love Jesus", we might well heed the warning of Professor Whitehead who said, "Mere ritual and emotion cannot maintain themselves untouched by intellectuality". We need to combine genuine reverence with intellectual integrity. The great danger facing Christianity is not its likely disappearance but its continued existence on a low level. This will be the case, unless a more demanding kind of intellectually responsible faith emerges in the Church of Christ. We live in an age of anti-intellectualism and it is an age that is largely ignorant of theology. Even religious leaders, such as a colleague of mine, tell us that they are not interested in theology, which is somewhat the equivalent of a doctor saying he isn't interested in medicine or a lawyer saying he isn't interested in the law.

Everyone who is intellectually and spiritually alive is liberal in the sense that he is open to truth wherever it comes from and wherever it leads. We owe much to the past, to our tradition, but we must not be bound by it. We speak of the church as a "living tradition", referring to the rich heritage that is ours, and we are grateful for that. But traditions are not always good. Sometimes they have been meaningful to our fathers, but their significance or usefulness have been lost through the years and they can hinder our progress in the church or in the community. During World War Two, I believe it was, an American artillery officer, stationed in England, observed their artillery maneuvers. He noticed that when each man took his position at the cannon, one man came and stood a short distance apart, but played absolutely no part in the firing of the artillery piece. When the American officer inquired about it, he discovered that this was the man who, when the cannon was pulled by horses, was the one who held the horses. Though there was no longer any need for that, because of tradition they still had him take his place.

We have respect for our heritage, the sacrifices which have given us what we have, the "blood, sweat, and tears" which have made not only the universal church what it is, but our own local church as well. We do not discount all that the dedicated men and women in our churches have done. But, in all its great periods, the Christian faith has been a revolutionary faith. We need warm hearts, certainly, but we need clear heads, too. Harry Overstreet once said an interesting thing about an American folk hero, the boy, "who stood on the burning deck whence all but he had fled." Mr. Overstreet remarked that the boy was not a hero but just a dumb cluck who could not adapt himself to a changing situation.

If our religion is to meet the needs of today's world, it must have at its very center our eternal contemporary, Jesus of Nazareth. He involved Himself in the human situation and that choice led to a cross. But, by taking up the burden of His brothers, he changed the course of human history forever. In religion, the only effective person in our complex world is one who sees that there is no conflict between the warm heart and the clear head. There must be in us a combination of straight thinking and deep devotion. We need to be aware of the real mission of the Church, not forgetting the commission of our Lord to go out into all the world with His Gospel. In His poem *If He Should Come,* Edwin Markham asks some questions which make us think:

> If Jesus should tramp the streets tonight,
> Storm-beaten and hungry for bread,
> Seeking a room and a candle light
> And a clean though humble bed
> Who would welcome the workman in
> Though He came with panting breath,
> His hands all bruised and His garments thin —
> This workman from Nazareth?
> Would rich folk hurry to bind His bruise
> And shelter His stricken form?
> Would they take God in with His muddy shoes
> Out of the pitiless storm?
> Are they not too busy wreathing their flowers
> Or heaping their golden store?
> Too busy chasing the bubble hours
> For the poor man's God at the door?
> And if He should come where churchmen bow
> Forgetting the greater sin,
> Would He pause with a light on His wounded brow,
> Would He turn and enter in?
> And what would He think of their creeds so dim,
> Of their weak uplifted hands,
> Of their selfish prayers going up to Him
> Out of a thousand lands?

There is much criticism of ministers dealing with social issues. Why don't they stick to the Gospel? Do they really understand the Christian Gospel? What of the prophets of the Old Testament? What of our Lord Himself? We have our Lord in our minds as a figure only of sweetness and light, not one who could have driven the money-changers out of the temple. The sweet portrayals of Jesus in art do not do justice to the powerful, conquering, loving spirit of one who came to bring life into the kingdom of death. Perhaps this is why we have a "Casper Milquetoast" religion. It makes no demands on us. When Epstein displayed His statue of the risen Christ pointing accusingly at the nail prints in His hands, looking out at all as if to ask, "why?", the sculptor met savage criticism. A priest said he looked like an Asiatic-American or a Hun. "He should have been portrayed with a beard", somebody said, as if Christ must be "dated". The sculptor said to his critics: "The traditional Christ in art harps on one element alone to the exclusion of all others. Sweetness and meekness are certainly present in that personality. But it is far more complex. The Gospels clearly show that there was intellect and power and a sense of justice as well." When the people in Jesus's times were hemmed in with Roman restrictions as well as the stifling effect of Hebrew ceremonial laws, Christ opened a door into a new freedom of the spirit. Even conservative New Testament scholars like E.F. Scott tells us: "We cannot recover the new Testament Church, nor is this desirable." Today, we need to build a Christian Church in terms, not of the first century, but of the twentieth.

We have members today in the Church of Jesus Christ, men and women and youth who are rich in intelligence and have a willingness to serve. We have money enough to support our church and make a worthy contribution to the church universal. But our passionate need is to cease bowing to a blank wall of tradition and follow the Christ of the 20th century. We need Him to sit in our pews and enlighten our worship. We need Him to linger in the halls of our learning and bring inspiration to our teachers. We need Him to dwell in our homes and cleanse our hearts. We need a Christ who will shatter our complacency, demolish the bigotries which threaten to strangle us, and who will comfort the sorrows of the heart. When this Christ of the 20th Century sits in our pews, only then we shall be a great Church. It will of necessity be a time when we have warm hearts and clear heads, what John Wesley said were the two great necessities: knowledge and vital piety.

XI

THE DEVIL MADE ME DO IT
(Sin and Salvation)

In these difficult days, when we are confronted not only with unemployment, the advent of "the new poor", inflation co-existing with recession, but also with the threat of nuclear annihilation of the race, we need to do more than blame those who are in power. We have every right to do that; but we need to take our individual share of the responsibility. Instead of blaming others, we need to look closely at ourselves to see where we have failed, through sins of omission as well as sins of commission. We need to remind ourselves that we are not saved by works, that it is only by the grace of God that any of us is saved. At the same time, we need to be aware that we often pass by on the other side, ignoring our neighbor's needs and the evils of our society, as well as our personal sins.

It is not through any merit of our own that we are saved. We are all unprofitable servants. God does not look at things in the same way that we do. We do not earn our salvation by accumulating points, as our children do when they get so many points for brushing their teeth or doing household chores. God is not an accountant. We are justified by faith, "not because of works, lest any man should boast". (EPH. 2:9) This God of Jesus whose forgiving love is so clearly revealed in the Cross of Calvary is always ready to forgive us when we come to Him in penitence, sorrow for our sins.

Our greatest temptation is to blame someone else for our sins and shortcomings. We so rapidly project our failures on someone else, even if it is something our mother did or did not do when we were children. The Transactional Analysts tell us that we should not listen to the "parent tapes"; that is, we should not continue to blame emotional or mental problems on our parents. But we are so inclined to blame others, to project our own shortcomings on someone else or some circumstances of life. The comedian, Flip Wilson, often said, when he did something that he should not have done, "the Devil made me do it." There is an element of truth in this, of course, in that there is in each of us a tendency toward evil. Some have called it "original sin", but most of us no longer believe that. However, the theologian, Reinhold Niebuhr, expressed this evil tendency in this way: "People are no damn good." The wide-spread waywardness of people in general bear out the truth of this statement. We are so inclined to blame everyone else and everything else for our sins and shortcomings; not only our parents, but also "the breaks", the signs of the Zodiac, lack of education or opportunity, anyone or anything else but ourselves. The mood of the times seems to be that no one wants to take responsibility for his own actions or failures. Freudian psychology has, perhaps, had something to do with it. For it is based on the premise that our complexes, obsessions and neuroses, psychotic behavior, are traceable to our childhood, so our parents are to blame. We should be grateful that the trend is away from that idea to that of individual responsibility. "If you feel guilty, you are guilty." But the attitude of "passing the buck" is still with us. Such as this from Goodman Ace's column in the *Saturday Review*: "Dorothy, your report card is very poor." "I know, Mother, but I've told you time and again that my Math, History, and English teachers all hate me, fanatically." Or "What do you mean by sneaking in here at eight in the morning? Where were you all night, young man?" "But, Dad, the prom broke up so late that I simply had to stay over at her apartment, because you wouldn't let me have the car last night." If anyone deserves punishment, it is the three teachers and the father. Never mind the fact that the girl hasn't cracked a book or shown the slightest interest in Math, History, or English or that the boy crashed into the garage door the last time he took the car. And, besides, he doesn't have a driver's license. However, buck-passing is not an invention of the young: "The devil made me do it." Mark Twain said he would like very much to meet the devil, because anyone who could hold the complete allegiance of nine-tenths of the world's population for so long a time must be a highly interesting and fascinating person.

In the desert long ago our Lord fought it out with the devil and won. Because He saw through and understood the problems of life that today are about as they were then. It began with bread (man's materialistic needs) which has always been so important. The communist philosophy is that if you feed men's bodies you will get their souls. "Man shall not live by bread alone", said Jesus, "but by every word that proceeds from the mouth of God." (Matt. 4:4)

There are two kinds of religion — the kind that looks to God to do things for us, the other looks to Him to do things *in* us and *through* us. The first does not make people good. Jesus came for the purpose of the latter, to bring people to God. Jesus rejected all magical religion, as witness his refusal to throw himself down from the high place. He rejected all the short-cuts.

Religious liberalism is sometimes guilty of making our Christianity costless by watering down and thinning out our faith. This is the great peril of liberalism, that for many people faith is so vague and indefinite that it is too easy. It costs nothing. When I graduated from seminary I was an avowed liberal. But, in the years since, though I have not forsaken it entirely, I no longer believe in the essential goodness of mankind. I have, however, tried to keep an open mind which is one of the trademarks of the true liberal. I have come to see, too, that social activism without the warm heart is not enough and that efforts to effect social change are ineffective unless the motivation is heartfelt religion that comes from surrender and dedication to Christ. It is, of course, inevitable that multitudes of people should go through this process. It was because they refused to believe something just because grandpa believed it. We had to get rid of a faith that was not intellectually sound, beliefs which insulted our intelligence. The result had been, in many cases, a vague, indefinite faith, so simple to believe that it makes little difference in the way we live. The faith in God and man which sent Christ to the cross had in it something dangerous and difficult. Such a faith need not insult one's intelligence, but it certainly is costly. It is a tremendous experience to believe in God as Jesus did. Man is God's highest creation and was given mastery over al the rest of creation. He is not only master, but trustee or steward, responsible to God for the use he makes of His gifts. God has made us, as the Psalmist said, "little less than God", (Psalm 8:5) but when we see the depths of human depravity, we can say with even deeper meaning, "What is man that thou art mindful of him?" (Psalm 8:4)

We mentioned that God's purpose in the making of men was the development of character. Without freedom, that could not be accomplished. Without the possibility of evil, there could be no such thing as good. Through free choice is the means of growth. Only the dedicated Christian is free; that is, because he is bound by his sense of responsibility to God.

Religion is not reserved for a separate compartment of our lives. It has to do with all of life. The late William Temple, archbishop of Canterbury, wrote in his book *Nature, Man, and God:* "If we make a total severance between God and the world, as between a carpenter and a box he has made, or to take Paley's famous illustration, between a watchmaker and a watch, we are on the way to that separation between sacred and secular which ends by making religion a special, peculiar interest in persons constituted in a particular way." This view of the compartmentalized life is not consistent with vital religion.

The eminent Psychologist Dr. Victor Frankl imprisoned by the Nazis in World War II, states: "The church is a hospital for sick souls, not a museum for the exhibition of saints." This is the answer to the critics of the church, such as those people who don't go to church because, they say, there are too many hypocrites in the church. After all, it isn't a matter of competition in being good. We are to help each other to become good; but, in the final analysis, I am, spiritually speaking, responsible only for my own soul's welfare. Emphasis on works, without the accompanying life of devotion, can lead to self-righteousness. How different it might be if the angry protesters were to heed the words found in *The Imitation of Christ:* "Be not angry that you cannot make others as you wish them to be, since you cannot make yourself as you wish to be." This is the danger in self-righteous pietism. The extreme pietist likes to sing "It is well with my soul", while the activist likes to sing "O Master, let me walk with Thee". Paul's position is that he cannot make the grace which loved him as of no effect; he must spend all life in one great endeavor to show how much he loves the God who loved him so much. That is the obligation of grace. Good works are the flowers which naturally spring from the soil made fertile by faith.

We should be much more concerned with making ourselves over than with trying to make other people over. The first thing we need to do is to pray God to give us the gift of seeing ourselves as others see us; and, more important, as God sees us. For Paul, the essence of the Christian life is to be "IN" Christ. In Galatians 2:20 he said: "I have been crucified with Christ; It is no longer I who live; but Christ who lives in me." And this is the crowning touch, as far as you and I are concerned: "Therefore, if anyone is *in* Christ, he is a new creation; the old has passed away, behold, the new has come." (II Cor. 5:17)

Most of us, who were brought up on ancient values we believe to be absolute and eternal are shocked by a "new" morality which, in reality, is not new. I share this negative view of the new morality, for the most part. However, it is a mystery to me how some people who think it is so terrible when it is applied to sexual behavior, pre-marital and extra-marital, but do not show the slightest pangs of conscience when it comes to racial discrimination or war, in spite of the fact that Jesus taught us to love our neighbor as ourselves and, too, we have the commandment "You shall not kill". (Matt. 5:21)

In 1966 an American professor, Joseph Fletcher, wrote a book called *Situation Ethics.* His basic premise is that there is nothing which is universally wrong, nothing intrinsically good or intrinsically bad. What we have to take to any situation is an act of judgment. There is only one thing that is absolutely, always, and universally good and that is love, the "agape" kind of love. We must in any situation work out what love is. Suppose, for example, a house catches fire and in it there is a baby and the original of the painting, the Mona Lisa. Which do you save? The baby or the priceless and irreplaceable picture? Of course you save the baby because a life is always of greater value than a picture. However, some decisions are not as clearly defined as this. With the situationist, there is no absolute right or wrong. We have to work it out in each situation.

Situation ethics, commonly known as the new morality, gives us a very great amount of freedom. One of the editors of the New York Times, James Reston, wrote: "No generation ever talked so much about commitment, yet seemed so unwilling to commit themselves to one man or woman, or one useful job of work . . . . They talk about 'participatory democracy' but most of them do not participate in the democratic process. They complain about the loss of individualism but run in packs. They condemn the welfare state but lean on it. And praise the good life and personal happiness but for all their activity, often seem bored and unhappy." As long as we live in this world we cannot avoid being involved in some things we do not approve, such as war. I can be absolutely opposed to the liquor business; but, whether I want to or not, I take money from it when the tax on liquor is used to pave streets or to educate our children: We are followers of an impossible goal in the life and teachings of our Lord, a moral standard impossible to achieve. Yet we, as Christians are bound to try. There are two answers, that of the absolutist or that of the relativist. Absolutism means making no compromise in trying to live by the moral code. The problem is that some of us are absolutists in one area and relativists in others. We may be absolutists when it comes to pre-marital sex, but not when it comes to racial segregation, for example. The relativist is more apt to compromise because he takes the attitude that, since there is so little he can do about the situation, there is no need to be concerned about it. It is society that has sinned. He is not responsible. Of course, that point of view ends in indifference to evil and to spiritual deadness. Most people would rather have their decisions made for them and have laws and principles to apply to the situation. As to our youth I believe they want rules and regulations. Dr. J. Wallace Hamilton said that the situation ethics takes too long for a couple to figure out in the back seat of a parked car. They need and want guidelines.

If all men were saints, then situation ethics would be the perfect answer. Since we are not saints, we need the protection of laws and principles. The proponent of the new morality is liable to forget the grace of God. Unless Christianity is totally false, then it must make good its claim to make bad men good. To encourage permissiveness is no real answer. To direct people to the grace of God is. We need to remember that the law consists of those values which the race has found to be a valid guide for living. Experience has shown them to be good. Our society has learned what are the values to live by and what is a threat to those values. Jesus, of course, has revealed the perfect code of ethics. One of the great problems today is to adjust that delicate balance between freedom and law and between the individual and society. The only real solution is for us to discover what it means to love our neighbor as ourselves..

There are certain standards of conduct that are absolute and unchanging. This does not mean that there are not times when we take into consideration all the facts in the situation before we make our decision as to what we will do; but there are some absolute standards and, if we live by them, we will automatically make the right decision without having to think it over. This is an acceptable kind of moral relativism. The other kind equates what is the right course of action with the mores of a particular point in time. I have the feeling that the greatest threat to our way of life is not communism, as threatening as that is, and it is not the John Birchers, or the hippies, or the anti-war demonstrators. It is the easy and casual compromise we are all making with simple human decency.

One of the most distinguished of the Christian intellectuals of our century who were responsible for reminding us of man's sinful nature was Reinhold Niebuhr. To him, sin is "inordinate self-love." But he doesn't stop there. Renewal is possible because, though all men are sinners, they are at the same time bombarded by the love of God. The living Christ stands at the door of every human heart and knocks. Blaise Pascal said: "The Christian religion, then, teaches men these two truths: That there is a God whom man can know. And that there is a corruption in their nature which renders them unworthy of Him." There is personal sin and there is social sin. We cannot escape either. We are all sinners. And we are all involved in the evils of society. Too many people are laboring under the false assumption that all men would be kind and good if only they were not corrupted by society. John Woolman, early Quaker anti-slavery leader, combined in his life both devotional experience and social concern. He was acutely conscious of the danger of a social witness that could have become hard and cruel in its denunciation of others.

Freedom and the dignity of man are inseparable. When there is no longer respect for the dignity of man, of each individual, the freedoms of democracy are gone. If the color of skin keeps a child from educational opportunities equal to those offered white children or if a man is condemmed through "guilt by association" by a Congressional Committee or a man is harassed because of different political opinion, real freedom is gone. Which is worse, communism or fascism? In the end result, there is no difference. Our Christian heritage, however, is based on the worth of the individual person. Not only should we be humble because all that we have we owe to God, but it is also true that we all need each other. We are dependent upon one another. As we have, in Paul's metaphor, many parts in our body, we are one body in union with Christ and we are all joined to each other as are the different parts of one body. The word "member" originated with Paul. When a member no longer performs its function, it is no longer a member. We are dependent on others; they are dependent on us. So we are to use our different gifts in accordance with the grace God has given us, whether to preach, teach, serve, whatever our talents may be. It is only as we give ourselves to the highest that we are truly free. Bound to God through the commitment of our lives to Christ, we are free to give expression to the best that is within us. In the words of the hymn:

"Holy Spirit Right Divine,
King within my conscience reign:
Be my Lord, and I shall be
Firmly bound, forever free."

We need to put ourselves in the other fellow's place, to be able as nearly as possible, to understand how he feels. A social worker has said that it is not the prosperous people, usually, who put coins in the blind man's cup. It is the underpaid clerks and others whom the blind man counts on most. This is because only those who have known what poverty is are able to empathize with him. That is how the Alcoholics Anonymous does its work. Only an alcoholic can reach an alcoholic. He has been there; he understands. I wonder if most young people have the slightest conception of what it means to get older and lonelier. And have the older people forgotten what it means to be young and to really understand the impatience of youth?

John Woolman, mentioned above, walked barefoot from Philadelphia to Baltimore. Why? So that he would know how the slaves felt when they had to walk that distance with bare feet. It was the spirit of Christ within him which gave him the incentive to do that. A Gentile newswriter who was to write an article on anti-Semitism, took a Jewish name and lived for months as a Jew. He found himself snubbed in certain social groups, was even refused a room in a hotel. Then he wrote a book to help us to feel the hurt and the humiliation suffered by Jews in some situations. In John's Gospel we read: "And the Word became flesh and dwelt among us". (John 1:14) Only by entering into the human situation could Jesus be real to us. It is because we know that He was subject to the same desires, fears, and temptations with which we are faced. So we know that He understands the constant battle we face in choosing between the forces of good and evil.

We speak of the generation gap, but there are other gaps, such as between the conservatives and the liberals in politics and religion. Sometimes there are closed minds on both sides. Those on the right, the conservatives, do not want the church to be relevant to the modern situation; that is, they do not want us "to meddle in politics", so some of them leave because the church is too relevant. On the other hand, the ones on the left, the liberals, want the church to be relevant; that is, to deal with social, economic, and political issues, to become involved in the present-day situation. Some of these people leave because the church is not relevant. Oft-times, social institutions can be best criticized and opposed by those who have been a part of them and know their weaknesses. An example is the way in which the Pharisees were attacked by Paul, a former Pharisee. In the same way, monasticism was attacked most successfully by Martin Luther who had been a priest. Our young people say that they are rebelling against the materialism of the older generation. It may be that, if they had lived through the depression, material things such as money and the things money can buy might mean more to them. There is really nothing wrong with material things, only their selfish use. If those people who control great wealth would come under the influence of the Spirit of Christ, as some do, they would be motivated to do something to remedy the economic inequalities and injustices.

The mood of the times seems to be that we do not want to take responsibility for our own actions or failures to do what we ought to do. As someone has said, we judge other people by their actions and ourselves by our intentions. Freudian psychology has probably contributed to the attitude of failing to accept one's individual responsibility for his faults. Freud traced our attitudes and actions to a great extent to our childhood, so our parents are to blame, as we have previously pointed out. It is a good thing, it seems to me, that the trend is in the opposite direction. To individual responsibility. In other words, "If, you feel guilty, you are guilty." The way of Christ is the only solution to our dilemma, the only way to solve our social problems. We, then, will cease blaming the devil, our parents, or our situation, for our failures. Jesus said: "For it is written, 'thou shalt worship the Lord your God, and Him only shall you serve.' " (Matt. 4:10) We condemn the young for their wanting to go their own way and perhaps we should. But they have many questions that we are not answering, because we, too, do not have the right set of values. Ours is a materialistic generation. All of us are going to have to find our answers in Him who loved us and gave Himself for us. If we are going to become what God wants us to be, we are going to have to follow Him who is "the way and the truth, and the life" (John 14:6) to get there.

In these troubled days we will not have peace even in our own land, unless we can learn to live together as brothers and work for the abolition of poverty, for the equality of all peoples, regardless of sex or race or any other consideration. We must get on with the business of making a better world and that can only come as we make better people. We who call ourselves Christians can only make other people better as we ourselves are redeemed and made better. The church must become a truly redemptive fellowship.

The Christian religion is a costly religion. Jesus said: "If any man would come after me, let him deny himself, and take up his cross, and follow me". (Matt. 16:24) This is a chaotic and desperate world in which we are living. And it will not be saved by crystal cathedrals or "peace of mind" religion or even by "possibility thinking". It will be saved only as you and I get out into the world "Where cross the crowded ways of life". The conclusion of the book mentioned previously, by Dean Kelley, titled *Why Conservative Churches Are Growing,* is that the narrow sects which insist on adherence to certain doctrines and are primarily concerned with "keeping oneself unspotted from the world" are growing faster than the more ecumenical churches which are more concerned with social evils. As for me, and I believe for the author, I would rather be in the latter group even if we are not growing as fast or if, in fact, we may be losing some members who think we have no business meddling with social evils. I would rather have an open mind than a closed one. The fact is, however, that there is no reason why the more liberal churches cannot have both service and devotion. Service without devotion is rootless. Devotion without service is fruitless. One can really complement the other. Religion must be more than a personal religious emotion. If the only element in religion is personal ecstasy, then the drug religion meets the test. Actually, it is not an either/or. Both elements are necessary, deep devotional life and social concern. "He who has the son has life" (I John 5:12). And that is as true in national and international relationships as in personal character. It is, of course, difficult to believe and to practice this kind of religion. But anything else is too easy. The center of Christianity has always been the cross. And that is because, in the long run, we do not want an easy religion. Rather, what we really want is a demanding religion that will take all that we have to give. That is the kind of religion we have in Christ and the Cross.

Dr. William Temple, late Archbishop of Canterbury, in his book, *Nature, Man, and God* wrote these significant words: "The true aim of the soul is not its own salvation; to make that its chief aim is to ensure its perdition, for it is to fix the soul on itself as center. The true aim of the soul is to glorify God; in pursuing that aim it will attain to salvation unawares." . . . (Lecture XV pps. 390, 391) . . . "The one hope of bringing human selves into right relationship to God is that God should declare His love in an act, or acts, of sheer self-sacrifice, thereby winning their freely offered love. Then all is of God; the only thing of my very own to which I can contribute to my own redemption is the sin from which I need to be redeemed. We are clay in the hands of the Potter and our welfare is to know it." (Lecture XV, pps. 400, 401, 402)

Various theories of the Atonement have attempted to explain the way in which man can be saved from his sins. The doctrine of redemption has had a large place in the theology of the church. The "ransom" theory was one of the first of these theories. In this theory, the question is "to whom is the price paid?" Early theology saw it as paid to the devil who held men captive. This theory has been questioned because it implies that the devil is a power that can or must be bought off even by God. One theory holds that the blood of Jesus, His sacrifice on the cross, paid for our sins, so all we have to do is accept Him. Another theory has been called the "satisfaction" theory, which holds that the death of Christ, the God-man, must be understood as a "satisfaction" paid to God for the sin of mankind by which His honor is offended. This theory has been criticized because of its view of the nature of God, that He should demand the death of a completely innocent man in order that His honor and justice be upheld. No Council or authoritative church body has ever produced an orthodox doctrine of the atonement. A later and, to me, more reasonable doctrine of the Atonement is that the contemplation of the Cross so moves the believer that he will see in it the transforming power of God's sacrificial love and thus be led to repent of his sins, devoting his life after this experience to a life of sacrificial love.

Even some of the reformers, such as Luther, saw the suffering of Christ as the divine punishment for the sin of the world, through either the "ransom" or "satisfaction" theories. This means that our Lord's sacrifice on the Cross was to placate either Satan or God. Most liberal thinkers in succeeding years have found the significance of Christ's redemptive work in the influence of His love and example, the moral influence theory. In the first place, it is a moral impossibility to transfer goodness or evil. And we certainly would be inclined on logical grounds, to reject the Dualism which pits God against Satan in the battle for the minds and hearts of men; because we do not, for example, believe in a personal devil as the personification of evil. We do, however, believe that there is an evil tendency in the lives of men. We prefer to believe that this power of evil or bent toward sin is the result of the freedom which God has chosen to give us. He has created us as free creatures with the opportunity to choose between good and evil. God did that because He is concerned with the making of men, the development of character. Without that freedom, we would be merely puppets with the strings in the hand of God. This is not the idea of God or of man which was revealed in Jesus Christ. Paul wrote in Galatians (5:13, 14): "For you were called to freedom, brethren; only do not use your freedom as an opportunity for the flesh, but through love be servants of one another. For the whole law is fulfilled in one word, 'You shall love your neighbor as yourself.' " Yes, love yourself as a child of God. And love your neighbor, too, for he is a child of God whom we can help, wherever he lives, whoever he is.

In John's Gospel we read: "And the Word became flesh and dwelt among us." (John 1:14) Only by entering into the human situation could Jesus be real to us. Only as we know that He was subject to the same desires, fears, temptations, to which we are subject. Thus, we know that He understands our human condition, the circumstances that surround our lives, the constant warfare within us between the forces of good and the forces of evil. It is the Suffering Love of God, revealed in Christ, that attracts us to the Cross. It is through no merit of our own, only through the Suffering Love of God in Christ that we are saved. I read somewhere (the source is not at hand) that in a book on Psychiatry is the story of an incorrigible boy. "In spite of all sorts of punishment, corporal, denial of things he liked, confinement, and so on, nothing was effective. Then, on a hot, summer afternoon, he was trying to teach his little pet dog a certain trick. When the dog did not respond as the boy thought he should, the boy kicked the dog in the mouth until it bled. Not understanding, the dog tried desperately to do the trick. Failing, he put out his blood-stained tongue and tried to lick the little boy's hand. The boy broke down. Blinded with tears, he ran sobbing to his mother. She said to him: 'Whatever is the matter?' 'I have done an awful thing,' he sobbed, 'I have done an awful thing.' Restrictions never made him cry. Beating never changed him, But suffering love did it. And that is only the suffering love of a little dog." We have available for us the Suffering Love of God, the greatest power the world has ever known, the Suffering Love which suffers and goes on loving until there is nothing we can do except surrender to it. One cannot stand in the presence of the Cross and truly understand its meaning without having his life transformed. That Suffering Love alone has the power to save man and to redeem His world from sin and death.